Body of History
NOW YOU SEE ME

GAY LE

Body of History
Now You See Me

Copyright © 2021 by Gay Le.

Paperback ISBN: 978-1-952982-83-5
Ebook ISBN: 978-1-952982-84-2

All rights reserved. No part in this book may be produced and transmitted in any form or by any means, electronic, or mechanical, including photocopying, recording, or by any information storage and retrieval system, without permission in writing from the copyright owner.

The views expressed in this work are solely those of the author and do not necessarily reflect the views of the publisher hereby disclaims any responsibility for them.

Published by Pen Culture Solutions   01/28/2021

Pen Culture Solutions
1-888-727-7204 (USA)
1-800-950-458 (Australia)
support@penculturesolutions.com

Contents

What Is Nirvana? vii
Introduction ix

Chapter 1   I Am Emotion 1
Chapter 2   I Am Cosmic 11
Chapter 3   I Am Evolution 23
Chapter 4   I Am Inequality 42
Chapter 5   I Am Divided 54
Chapter 6   I Am Nation 71
Chapter 7   I Am Karma 86
Chapter 8   I Am Lying 100
Chapter 9   I Am Imbalance 121
Chapter 10 I Am Rebuilding 133
Chapter 11 I Was Your Keeper 137
Chapter 12 Avant-Garde Me 160
Chapter 13 I Was Victim 179
Chapter 14 The Diabolical Path 192
Chapter 15 I Was Splendid 201
Chapter 16 I Am Injustice 219
Chapter 17 I Was Blind 234
Chapter 18 Reincarnational Continuum 246

Now Can You See Me? 249
Index Of Images Pixabay 251

What Is Nirvana?

The student asks his Guru "What is Nirvana?"

His teacher responds "Whatever you perceive it to be."

"But master once you perceive something it becomes that perception," answers the student quite perplexed.

"That is true,' answered his guru.

"If Nirvana is simply my perception of what I think it is, then where do you go when you meditate?"

His master starts laughing "nowhere," his master continues laughing and laughing

This perplexes the student even more. "Why do you laugh Master," he queries?

"What's your next question" laughs the guru?

The student had to think about it "what's nowhere?"

"Now you have asked. Now through your perception it is somewhere." He laughs.

"But I'm still confused master."

"Don't ask my son; don't ask." His master vanished.

Many years passed and this quandary still puzzled the student.

Then the spark of Nirvana struck him.

You already have everything you want and need.

It is in the asking that you shall receive. All of it, in opposite and equal value.

He laughed as he understood. Nirvana means; "don't ask!"

For it is in experiencing all that it isn't, that you understand all that it is:

By Gay Le, 2020

Introduction

You have to experience all that it isn't; to understand all that it is

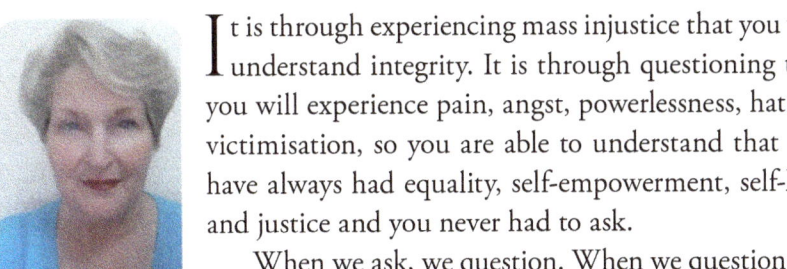

It is through experiencing mass injustice that you will understand integrity. It is through questioning that you will experience pain, angst, powerlessness, hatred, victimisation, so you are able to understand that you have always had equality, self-empowerment, self-love and justice and you never had to ask.

When we ask, we question. When we question, we are answered. When we pursue, we receive. However, you will always undergo that which you do not wish to experience for you to acquire that which you do not understand.

When scanning the world around you, the answer to all your questions is before you. You created your environment through reactions. You are re-living your responses over and over again. By appraising your results, you now have all your answers. By experiencing the injustice, you understand justice; by experiencing inequality, you understand equality; by experiencing powerlessness, you understand self-empowerment, by experiencing the cold-heartedness of hatred, you now understand the exuberance of love.

When reaching this point of realisation, you understand you have already experienced all these emotions for thousands of years and you know how they all end. You also understand that by empowering one emotion is asking. In asking, you will always receive. In receiving you will always experience the answer to the opposite and equal value for you to understand every component of your question.

You already have everything you will ever require. You will never need justice for you always had it.

Relax; Allow; "Don't ask!"

Gay Le, 2020

Chapter One

I AM EMOTION

NOW SEE ME

The universe is comprised of zillions of cells. When a group of specific cells coagulate together a shape, a colour, a density, is formed creating everything from the smallest insect to the largest galaxy.

Every one of these cells has a binary code and every code has to match and syncopate with the universal matrix. Nothing is a mistake; Everything throughout the entire universe is perfectly balanced.

We as humans have an emotional format and every individual emotion is translated into binaries. We, as humans are no more than walking, talking, sculptures of 7 billion nano emotions embodied in human forms.

As there is no actual proof of the original binary of the universe however, we can only assume it would look something like 01 or 012. Zero always being God for it exists in all the binaries of all things.

The original human or Adam and Eve would be defined as the emotional binaries of 0111 male and 0112 female to the 100th zillion. Because they are the basic emotional codes, they would also exist in every code that is in existence today. Their binaries are the corner stones of our physical existence as emotional beings.

This is what I have based this component of my research on. The possibilities that the "instinctual survival psyche" within the original Adam and Eve's binaries are responsible not only for our individuality today but also many of the narcissistic behavioural patterns that exist throughout history.

In recent research it was discovered that not only did a Neanderthal man exist after the ice ages but there was another species called the hairless white man. This species designed spears and fished, making him more intellectually advanced, more physically adaptable and far more dangerous than any other life species on earth. Evidence also states that this species advanced inland, across most of Europe and further, copulated, over-populated and almost exterminated all other living species into extinction.

Many of these little populaces out of desperation returned to the sea and fish bearing areas. They became nations in their own rights however, in my narrative I adopt one of these titanic barbarian races and christen them as my first civilisation race of Adam and Eve. I cross reference much of my populace with my study of history.

I have not given them a breed nor a nation for they are the emotional binaries of all existences and they exist in all races. They are our evolutionary body of history.

They developed physically mentally and spiritually. They developed fishing skills, boating skills, warrior skills, religious philosophies, politics, and become renowned and feared among all their adversaries.

Due to their massive power and physical strength, the men saw themselves as Gods among men.

They saw and emotionally felt the rest of the world as inferior, weak, smaller, lessor. They created myths and legends to support their philosophies. They divided their world into three dimensions. Above us, below us and us. They believed the world to be flat and if they sailed too far, they would fall of the edge. They believed the earth to be the centre of the universe.

They discovered that if they fornicated with a woman when she was pure and when she was ovulating, she would breed him strong sons. If they copulated regularly with the females, they would breed females. They never married. They bought and sold the females like everything else, as property. They bore males as warriors; they bore females as breeding stock for more males. Everything was emotionally based on survival instincts.

Even though the laws of reincarnation didn't theoretically exist during this time, they still physically existed.

The reincarnational timeline suggests throughout history every time a dictating supremist or narcissistic leader deemed reasons to invade any other country, the truth was always hidden in the fallacies of their dominance. History has documented time and time again the basic reason for all foreign invasions is the emotional desire for power and greed; so, in reality the invaders always lied and this timeline of emotional injustice has been repeated and relived over and over again since the beginning of human time.

The next in line is the predator or warrior, otherwise known as the enabler. They obeyed their narcissistic leader blindly and proceeded to genocide, desecrate, violate and destroy their neighbour and their neighbour's property and claim it as their own for leader, God and country.

The victims of these onslaughts were usually weaker innocent beings; women children, babies, different ethnical groups, natives, different colours; they were murdered, imprisoned or forced into some form of slavery to this domineering regime.

They in turn were emotionally determined to seek their revenge. This is the third component of the cycle. The emotional hating of both the leaders and the perpetrators for their unjust actions, thus mirroring both.

This is the ongoing cycle of karmic restitution. Narcissist or instigator, followed by predator or enabler, then victim then back to being the instigator. This is the foundation of our karmic existence today.

They may experience three to four lifetimes to acquire all this but they, through their original superior feelings of dominance will experience future lives as an instigator, predator and victim. They experience their original feelings of emotional injustice to the opposite and equal value as originally perpetrated. They did all this to themselves repeatedly.

Because the law of karma is simply a biological program of balance, the progression of life's activities forges you forward through every existence and you receive, exactly as you gave, to opposite and equal value of what you gave in your previous life.

This emotional reincarnational concept is the keystone to our repeated ongoing human existences. When you understand that everything around you was done by you, to you and for you; you then comprehend that in harming others, you are actually only harming yourself.

With each perpetration of violence to any other being whom through your ego's judgement, you deemed or felt lessor than yourself; you in turn, because you have emotionally envisaged the entire scenario, will walk the entire path of your emotional judgement and experience every intricate and insignificant binary emotion.

If you are a white man and you spear a native, you in turn will eventually become that native and endure exactly the same injustice of path of the spear in your back.

When the first white supremist breed inhabited the earth there were less than 20000 people in existence. What they didn't understand was, every single human on the earth at that time was a mirror image of their cellular selves. This information indicates that within him and her, every cell was made up of 20000 different variations of emotions.

Each person may not have physically appeared the same; they may not have the same ethos; but they were all made up of exactly the same cellular structure and as such, emotionally acted and reacted in exactly the same manner. Everyone was equal to every other being upon the earth and all things throughout their existence because we are all designed the same way.

Exactly the same manner that you are designed and equal to all the stars in the Milky way. You are made up of exactly the same cellular formulas, the same cells with all the same universal information; you are simply moulded differently. Every living and nonliving creature is created this way. We all have exactly the same information in every cell of our body throughout the universe. We are like zillions of Lego pieces constructed into a universe, only we are binary. Every binary code is an individual emotion. We are physical embodiments of all those emotional binary codes.

When you abuse another person be it physically mentally or spiritually you are abusing that mirror image within you. The emotional injustice you feel within you now alters your binary, which alters your genetic codes. This starts to alter your chromosomes immediately, until that inner image you abused now transforms your outer physical appearance.

You physically embody that new emotional injustice. You are what that emotional injustice looks like.

We genetically explain our ethnical cultures from full breed to quarter caste in a forward descent. Reincarnations continuum explain ethnic descent, backwards from quarter blood, to half-caste to three quarter blood to full blood. You transform backwards with each existence from whom you are now to who you chastised or humiliated in each existence until you wear that physical resemblance.

That is why every thought, word and action is for and about you. You use these instruments to generate you to evolve.

Today there are 7 billion people on earth; 7 billion emotional mirror images of you in one form or another. They are feedback of all your emotional injustices you have experienced in your past and will experience in your future paths. They are feedback of your body of history. They are explaining all the life situations you have lived, survived and instigated throughout the past 200000 years. They also reveal the future path you have created for yourself to experience.

You have been African, Asian, European, English, Mid-Eastern, Viking, Aztec, Inca, Mediterranean, Native American, Indian both Asian and American, Aboriginal, Irish, Scottish, the list is endless. You have been male, females, child, rich man, poor man, beggarman, thief; fat skinny, strong, weak, wise and not so wise, married, single, abused accused and misused, loved and adored.

Every person on earth has binary codes just as you do, all with the same information as you do, in different ratios. Your binary codes although the same have similar readings but different ratios as they do and you are a part of them. They are now as much a part of you as you are a part of them, equally.

All binary codes alter your genetic codes and chromosomes to deliver all of you here at this moment in time because you are all one in the evolutionary path. Together we all progressed from Neanderthal man to Nuclear man as a world.

Our original warriors, Adam the narcissistic supreme annihilators, deemed all things to be lessor than them due to their titanic strength. Adam saw himself as liken to the Gods and thus had the right to take anything he wanted because he could and if others as in Eve's didn't submit, he could and would destroy them like he did to other nations.

This is the genus of the duality; the narcissistic egocentric personality; the Adam verses Eve the predator verses victim. This information is an intricate part of our original emotional binary codes. This is our original ego our original need to survive. These personalities are the basic formula of human existence throughout history and today.

Our children and those younger than us have progressed further as you will see. One person does not progress alone. They progress as a union, together as a generation, equally with the same understanding and capabilities. We are equal and as one. They are our future.

As a generation in the sixties, we acquired televisions bringing the outside world into our houses. As a generation in the eighties my children acquired and aspired to computers, taking our houses out to the world.

As a generation of the millennium my grandchildren are so much more technologically orientated and advanced and they were born this way as a generation. We evolve in generational groups. We see our past in the generations of our elders; we see our future in the generations of our children.

In the mid twentieth century when scientists divided the atom, researchers discovered that before they divided the atom it had 5 billion cells within it. After they divided the atoms, each atom still had 5 billion cells within them. Every time you divide a cell it reappears with exactly the same quantity of cells as it originally had. However, it was a brand new fully developed cell. When you cut yourself, your cells are cut in half. When your wound heals all those new cells are complete and whole again. We are embodiments of zillions of cells; we are immortal; we regenerate.

The original single cell creature in the water of the earth for zillions of years before we ventured on land evolved and duplicated itself. The laws of Fibonacci declare that this cell instinctually kept on duplicating and evolving then ventured to land.

When the Adam populace first made their appearance, there would have been an estimated 20,000 beings upon the entire earth. Every time they divided a cell it duplicated; they both returned reading the same information with the same impact and mirroring each other. Now 200000 years later there are 7 billion mirrored replicas of that first Adam and Eve nation. Their original binary of 0111+ has been duplicated 7 billion times and is within each and every one of us.

Our challenge is; our instinctual binary still indicates that you must fight to survive. You still believe you are an individual and everyone on earth is separate from you and has a pecking order.

If your psyche or feelings are divided within you, then your world is divided outside. This is the path of Adam and Eve. You will not understand true equality in any world until your worlds are united. There is only one path to freedom.

The world is the way it is, divided, separated, disorientated, because your feelings dictate the same manner of inequality. It is only when we experience all our past life disfunctions and understand what peace is, will you truly understand this experience.

This truth is you always had it; you simply do not know how to empower it.

"WE ARE HEALED OF ALL SUFFERING ONLY BY EXPERIENCING IT TO THE FULL." Proust.

The perception of heaven and earth are emotional fantasies within our consciousness. They are both a state of utopian peacefulness. We imagine how they would feel within us then believe they exist that way outside of us. Many people claim to want to go to heaven because they do not want to stay here. They dislike the injustice in the world.

However, they are the ones creating their injustice and preventing themselves from experiencing their heaven, because emotionally they are doubting, asking. Now we have true understanding; we can rectify that belief.

Past life regressions, life between life hypnotherapy were tools equivalent to time travel. However, we don't need to have a hypnotherapist transcend us. Through awareness today, we can realise we are actually re-living each past life existence every day. We keep reliving our past in loops. With our daily feedback we are now able to uncover many of the old obstructions that are hindering us. We are now able to uncover patterns and ongoing algorithmic equations that pave the way to real resolutions.

With these new solutions we are able to create futures without impoverishment, wars, violence.

We can create worlds of equalised growth and peace. All these paths were out of our grasp before, because we believed we were divided and separated. With these new empowering formulations, we are now thinking with our brains and not our brawn. We are learning to allow instead of react.

We are able to not only recognise our past paths but our future paths as well. We are also for the first time in creation as a united world able to rectify both paths and create a better world for us and future generations to exist in.

Recent research discovered with the bushfires in Australia now plays an integral part in my future development of the path of the reincarnation continuum.

This remarkable discovery through computerised technology, uncovered data displaying a path of predetermined gases and chemicals from reactions of specific trees. It disclosed the future path of the fire, days in advance. The blaze of the fire followed the gaseous channels of destruction. The researches also learnt that different colours of the data unearthed the predetermined intensity of the fire through specific areas.

This research was vital for the Australian environmentalists but, it was also poignant to my research as well, for its data physically and visually exposed how all future evolutionary paths are predestined and generated long before they are experienced.

All our inevitable paths are already determined; tomorrows crossword puzzle will be finished regardless of what I am doing today. How I finish it and when I finish will be my journey.

More inevitable facts are; in four billion years' time the Milky Way will collide with the enormous galaxy of Andromeda. Will earth survive? Of course not. In comparison we are less than space dust. The radiation incursion alone will annihilate our planet long before we enter its orbit.

These paths are already determined through past reactions of the universe billions of years go. It is now simply a path. It is how we emotionally react to the various situations surrounding us that determines the enjoyment or lack thereof, of each path. This is the same conception as the gaseous path predetermined for the fire.

Through our evolutionary path of 200000 years our narcissistic emotions of Adam and Eve within us has also evolved. Through his ingenuity he created spears; now he has also created nuclear weapons and atomic bombs, impoverishment, desecration of life, land, injustice, hatred and inequality.

The emotions these two individuals represent still instinctually fight to survive as the supreme invincible beings and they still incessantly divide our inner psyche, dividing our world around us. They empower one emotion over all others.

As long as we neglect to understand our binary embodiment of emotions, we will never find our true self-empowerment or our true freedom. Our justice, equality, self-empowerment, and self-love has always been within us; quietly allowing. They never emote the feeling of asking. They simply allow and it all comes to you; for they know we already have all the answers and everything we need with in us. We as emotional beings, just keep asking.

*You have to experience malevolence of duality,
To appreciate the benevolence of the allowance*

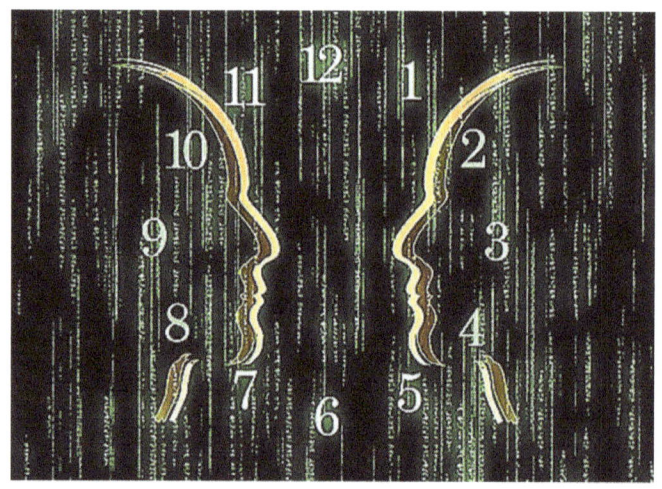

I WAS EMOTION

NOW CAN YOU SEE ME?

Chapter Two

I Am Cosmic

NOW SEE ME

To transform into this woman, I am today, my body of history has revealed that I have had to walk some horrendous terrains. I have had to confront many aspects of self both in this life and my past that I could have shrugged off and shoved under the carpet and continued on my merry way blaming others and ignoring the truth; but apparently, this time, that was no longer going to be the case. This time I will truly be awakened and learn how to unite my inner psyche.

Many components of this book may offend, but they are all my research put into practice and backed with proof. I alone re-walk my paths, constantly re-uniting my duality and constantly awakening my self-empowered Eve within me every chance I get. I am only responsible for my path. I cannot walk anybody else's path for them. I am not responsible for your decisions nor your reactions; you are.

However, in understanding the empowerment of allowing I do have an enthusiasm to excel within me, to achieve excellence for a better existence for all of me and those around me who follow me in this experience.

Because I am trained in the awareness of the reincarnational continuum and how history repeats itself, I ask myself; when others had this information, and I wanted to know it, what would I have wanted them to do with it. The answer was clear. I would have wanted them to share it with me and others so we all can understand it equally and experience it to the fullest.

When I started presenting my seminars some of the audience would ask, where could they get this form of information? The answer was, it was in the universities where PhD's and Doctorates study, but unavailable to the general public.

I realised I had at my disposal information and proof of our analysis and although I don't have a responsibility to inform all beings of future possibilities and probabilities, what I do have is the opportunity to explain how by altering our attitude, the objectives that are facing us at the moment can be perceptionally altered and how through this simple adjustment, we can enhance our lives now for the better and program more abundant livelihoods for future generations.

Simply by creating a new visual path is not the answer, that is asking. Firstly, we have to realise why the path we are undertaking is the path we are experiencing. That *question* has been asked by every individual at one time or another. Many different answers have been explained and divulged by motivational speakers only to gain a superficial momentary solution, but not the entire truth.

From the results of my latest analysis, we are developed enough to now be able to synchronise our past duality with our present moment then allow and empower the true paths we wish to experience. This is the information I offer. That is all I can do; the rest is up to you.

You will not understand what the wonderment of GOD is, until you experience all that GOD isn't.

In all my writings I express my beliefs of MY God. This path I took was for me. I shall explain my new allegiances and the reasons I came to these conclusions.

But lets' get one thing very clear, I am not a heretic. I am not a heathen. I am not some spiritual guru. I am a free born woman who has found MY TRUTH, because the bigoted duality of the God being offered to me simply wasn't good enough.

Due to misconceptions introduced by the Adam and Eve race, who, at the time were basing their belief systems upon their then culture; much of their myths, legends, philosophies and politics have eked throughout all of history, philosophy and religions.

Anatomical astronomical, binary sciences however for me today have divulged a path that is more formidable and practical and I'm more comfortable with where this new development will now lead me.

After reading and listening to endless systems of beliefs filled with the same derogatory remarks dating back over 20000 centuries; then studying all my reincarnational research along with NDE's, life between life and regressions, I was able to make one of the biggest decisions of my life.

I discovered why as a woman when I fought back before this century I was always physically abused. I discovered why I am now capable of standing up this century and not being knocked down, thus giving me the right to make more discerned decisions for me.

In the late 20th century, for the first time in history, I as a woman, was allowed to alter my past life time allegiances without being physically abused. They were and are the cause of all my ongoing extenuating circumstances in each of my existence.

I have studied various different religious philosophies over the years and come to the conclusion that the emotional binaries attached to the Judean/Christian/ Latin Roman /Hebrew God doesn't serve my purpose as a woman. They were the original instinctual binaries of Adam and Eve. These male orientated philosophies were intricately structured to serve the purpose of the self-absorbed few who prejudiced doctrines for self-preservation.

With today's new research and information, I have not only discovered that the binary of God is in every living thing, but that all things are created equal.

When a woman questioned in the past, she was chastised and physically abused or even murdered. Dictatorial elders would inform the husband to "get his house in order" which basically meant physically and violently abuse the female spouse/child into submission.

Up until 1960's or later in some countries, this action was still doctrinated and carried out by families, churches, politics and schools alike.

Pat Robertson in the sixties stated "you cannot allow women to be liberated. They will divorce their husbands, murder their children, become witches, become lesbians and destroy capitalism."

From the 1970's onward, men were no longer allowed to physically abuse any other being, male, female or child within their own home or elsewhere. It became an illegal offence.

Women were now not only allowed to be educated but were allowed to utilise that education to further advance their families, their homes, their careers and their personal lives.

At the turn of the millennia the study of Narcissism became available and now we had a name for all the past life discriminatory acts that have cursed all beings in every life time.

All the old philosophies have been heralded from our original Adam and Eve binary and what a religious deity should appear like over 200000 years ago.

So, the old men, elders, posed HIM, as an old huge muscular warrior sitting up on some daunting throne up in the clouds, like Zeus or Odin. This selective deity was dictating rules to the righteous male warriors. Only the magnificent warrior specimens who were recreated in HIS image understood his principles. These male Gods also fornicated with the most beautiful of human females giving birth to titanic demi Gods.

These monstrously titanic beings celebrated life with extreme exuberance. Their food kills, their drink and their fearless hunting and their relationships were all reprehensible and provocative. It was nothing for a male to grab a woman, sit her on his lap, have his sexual way with her, then throw her back into the crowd, while he was drunk and still eating dinner.

This is what Gods do. The celebrate victory ravishingly. No one questioned it. It was natural. It was their culture and they overly enjoyed all of the revelries of their successes as a celebration to their God, their King, believing HIM to have their backs in battle.

Centuries later in other territories, in many monastic temples, the archimandrites described this audacious behaviour as unbecoming. It was seen as vulgar, raucous and promiscuous. Many papyrus scripts written then translated this behaviour as immoral. However, it is through these ignorant celibate interpretations that Eve became the insalubrious lusciousness of a demon inciting the innocence of the male. Eve was then classed as the abomination, repugnant, and infested with bile's of humors.

These written indignations toward the female and lower gender continued for over 20000 years and were later re-enforced as law by the various puritanical authorities who instigated their God to be male orientated only and as such, man must deem themselves to celibacy, so as not to become intoxicated or infected by these vermin. These were monastically educated male children to abbots.

They were not farmers. The farmers were less educated, less value than they. The abbots knew nothing of how creation and nature worked. They scribed for many centuries that women and women alone created their own impregnations. This civilised and ignorant fallacy continued well into medieval times.

As a result of this uneducated indignation and mis- interpretation, girls as young as 12 were raped by roman soldiers then stoned to death. Babies were raped and murdered as they were soul-less property. Young girls were raped and burned to the stake to relieve them of their demons because some old paedophile was having fantasies about her.

If either parent stood up to defend their child, they too would be burned to the stake because the mother was the cursor of the child's fate. If you had twins, you were a witch. In the middle and late twentieth century young Slav girls were still being poisoned as experimental lab rats so scientist could diagnose the toxic reactions. Radiation poisoning carried out on islanders for they were perceived as lessor beings.

As opposed to the original Adam and Eve credo where women who created women were valuable, this purist celibate credo dictated that all other secular beings, especially women were created from flesh therefore, soul-less, godless, brainless, mindless, and worthless slaves.

These bigoted, sexist, racist, unprincipled biased instructions were to become the indoctrinated truths of the Latin Roman and future christian belief systems that donned the world up until the late1970's

Now there is proven researched data indicating that through our binaries in every cell of our body there are billions of fractal codes. These codes not only reveal your paths but the entire paths of all the universes. They reveal the most powerful sources throughout the entire universe, not just earth, and it is **ALL** a part of all of us.

This evolutionary information revealed that, like everything throughout the universe, we are nothing more than mega intricate universes ourselves, formulated from zillions upon zillions of cells. Every single one of those cells has the original GOD code or *A CREATION CODE*, and everything we need to live in perfect balance and harmony with all things throughout your body and entire multiple universes.

What this vital piece of information revealed was one small intricate cell in a droplet of blood in your body is equivalent to the same cells that are in the Milky Way or Andromeda. There is only a lot more of them and they are structured differently. You are equal to everything in the universe as one. This is my God.

This is my ONENESS.

When duality merges as one; nothing exists:
However, from the nothingness comes everything.

This phenomenal majesty supplies my *every* desire. That is the magical *wondrousness* of it.

However, this phenomenal majesty supplies my *every* desire; that is also the magical *entrapment* of it.

Everything you want and need has already been provided for you throughout the entire universe but my God CANNOT do it for me; for to do that is to divide and to divide is unfair and unjust thus creating victimisation and injustice. My God does not empower any emotions over another. That is human duality.

You screw up, desire or emotionally ask, there will be consequences. Karmic consequences; cause and effect. Cause is equal to the opposite effect to the same and equal value. However, when you are ready to understand, all will be magically revealed to you. That's karmic balance.

That is where we as humans seriously differ. We as emotional beings are writhing with feelings of superciliousness, egocentricity and narcissism. We empower the duality of inequality and injustice. We judge and question all things according to our own rules and belief systems.

Then we instinctually presume ourselves supreme and place everyone else in our perceptional little boxes and force them to abide by our rules, as our victims and if they don't, we challenge or manipulate them into submission.

Then when the "***fit hits the sham,***" we scream for HELP! expecting some contemptuous being, sitting on top of some cloud to save our supercilious arses from our now out of control dilemmas, which we produced, for us to endure.

I'm not informing people to alter their religious beliefs, that is their choice, I'm simply informing you that if you want to burn me to the stake, get in line. I deliberately chose my new path, because, the narcissistic duality being offered to me was dividing my inner house, creating centuries of antagonism and distress and was completely unsuitable.

Man's biblical and religious God has been created from many different and varied **man's** perceptions of who they want their God to appear like. Man, not God, christened Eve and coloured beings, people of ethnic diversity as worthless, whores, slaves. Beings who are physically, sexually lower and soul- less, and as such, the subordinate class that have had to bow down to these old narcissistic primitives and obey these arrogant forms of homosapien.

They divided themselves into both venerating and contemptuous beings. Their teachings although spoken outwardly were actually confessions of their true inner emotional injustices. The more they spoke, the more they revealed the original compulsive binary path of Adam and Eve within them. "The survival of the fittest instinct."

Eve have to be subservient to man, in whatever shape he takes, be it politician, banker, pope, monarch, husband, brother, uncle, teacher, priest, for according to these biblical instructions, she, in any form other than white supremist civilised educated male, was godless, did not have his soul, therefore, she had no rights.

To love Eve as a woman or have sex with her, the husband, or lover, must by law of this man's biblical teachings, be repulse by her for she was the very abomination of Satan himself.

Later post medieval doctrines disclosed that the **only** reason for fornication within a marriage with a woman was, for the reproduction of the ***male*** species only. Eve's were unsuitable. This doctrinated practice is still dominant in many Middle Eastern and Eastern cultures today. Unlike the Adam and Eve myths, where women were also indispensable, the celibate interpretation of females were, they are curs to be bought and sold off like beasts and then only according to their family genetic strength for the betterment of male species only.

That is one of the reasons why same sex marriage is so frowned upon from this form of bigotry. According to this apathetic dogma, they are in league with some sort of satin; for they are having sex for the sake of having sex and that is deemed as the sin of the flesh, and not reproduction and that is aberrant and they are doomed to some eternal damnation of hell.

For thousands of centuries Eve has been labelled as the brunt of all Adam's emotional injustices. She is the mongrel of all his anguish, the husband's property like cattle, sheep, housing, and land. Even though the words have altered, the basic doctrine still taught in many a church and temple is the serving of everyone and everything to the white supremist civilised educated male. Adam still rules with the iron fist.

Norse gods, Vikings, Celtic, Judean, Hebrew, Buddhism, Hinduism, Christianity, Church of England, Lutheran, Middle Eastern, Koran; 4200 different religions available today and a high percentage of them dictate the servitude of what is called the lower sex and breeds. You name the text you'll find the same deplorable plot originally designed from the Adam's male perception of what they believed their God should represent.

My acuity of my God is oneness, the all that already is. The empowering infinite probabilities of endless possibilities. In duality you ask, then play one emotion against the other; to understand one you must experience the other to its intensity; love, hate, inequality, equality, justice, injustice.

In My God's eyes, I am an all-amazing being, co-joined with 7 billion other amazing emotional binaries on earth within me. My body of history has evolved into this remarkable woman because of all my past. The injustices, regardless of their true intent transformed me into who I am. I am more than worthy and I have learnt to embrace my narcissistic Adam and my victim Eve for without them I would not be the inspirational self-empowering Eve that I feel I am today.

By understanding the importance both of these bohemians of emotional injustice played in my finding my true self, due to experiencing the barbaric paths they both provided for me, the magnificence of true Eve was revealed.

It is through this magical manifest of what I believe now, that I am now able to *feel* all the genuine love and empowerment supplied to me from my future inevitable path of joy, happiness and prosperity.

Once I recognised that every being upon the earth is informing me of all my emotional inequalities, past and future, I started allowing all my coloured equivalents to my white narcissistic Adam, my Irish equivalent to my Mediterranean and European, and my British equivalent to my aboriginal, Indian, native and Polynesian. Then I became the best of all of them and united them all as me. This is my oneness; this is my equality; this is my self-empowerment. I am nothing without them; I am all that is, with them all.

I feel eminently empowered and I feel myself as one with all beings. I experience this same equality outside of me, by allowing you all to exist as you want.

To ask for anything is to activate and empower the duality component of you that you are questioning. In other words, you will receive. You will experience what it isn't, to understand what it is.

I generate the art of allowing for me to experience the same in return. Instead of chasing emptiness, I allow everything to come to me.

If you sit across the table from me and complain of how bad your life is; I realise we are re-living a past regression. I see me in the mirror of my past as the victim. In understanding the karmic path, I now realise I can alter my future path.

By understanding what I see and hear, I can now choose to be a remarkable person who has overcome amazing obstacles. Through you I now see before me the victimising injustice I had to endure to become me.

You are telling me I have one more obstacle to overcome, another variety of victimisation. I have a choice for both of us. This is your future path as well as mine. If I choose to ignore it, we will continue on this same path. What would you want me to do? What do I choose to do?

By understanding how remarkable and brilliant we are to have walked such a path and I understand I must be brave too, I can now choose not to be a victim. I can choose for us both to walk a better path.

I realise I already know how this path ends; you have told me. Why would I choose to continue? I choose non-victimisation.

I inwardly embrace our encounter and the friendship of my companion, because out of 7 billion people in the world today if she had not taken the path she had taken, exactly the way she took it, I'm the one my companion chose to have coffee with to reveal our obstruction and that makes her exceptional.

The reason I explain this is because all my proclivities are determined from this perspective. If you disapprove, burn the book now.

I won't feel it; the world won't feel it; the universe won't feel it; but you will, through your feelings of superior judgement and fear of my beliefs and that very act of defiance will activate the duality within you and it will be your ongoing path. You will keep re-living it at the same time with the same impact in each existence until you stop.

Your emotional perception or your feelings toward my interpretation of my cosmic affiliations is an emotional feeling of some injustice initiated by your inner Adam. Be it justice or injustice is irrelevant. Adam has always deemed himself as superior; it's another survival instinct.

That emotional feeling is now your desire and be it hate, laughter, fear, political or religious diversification, this emotion is in every single cell throughout your entire body and these results will transform YOU physically into the embodiment of that emotion of injustice.

You are exactly the same as all cells in all the people around you; all the cells in the stars and all orbital universes surrounding you; all your binaries match. It's your inflated binary Adam ego of who you think you are, that falters your true identity. You are not superior to any one; you are not inferior to anyone; you are a miniscule binary cell, reacting to your feelings of your superior godhead initiated through this original binary.

The true hologram of you is zillions of cells of you in magical colours. Your consciousness has the capability of translating those colours from every individual person on the planet into different visuals of human form, thus creating the illusion of separation, individualism.

However, now ask a dog or cat or a bird what you look like? Their answer will surprise you.

Here however, is the irony. Man has the self-importance to presume the animals have it all wrong.

We need to learn to embrace all who are on earth for they are all our live past life re-experiences. The old and cranky, the obese and waif, the disabled and athlete, along with your Adam and Eve. They are all component of every existence you ever had and you are reliving your experiences with them again.

Find discontent with any of them, you find discontent within you. Now you will continue to experience that karmic effect of discontent in ongoing opposite and equal value until the lesson is learnt.

I AM COSMIC ONENESS

NOW CAN YOU SEE ME?

Chapter Three

I AM EVOLUTION

NOW SEE ME

Darwin's theory of "evolution by natural selection" states, "the strongest shall survive." Over centuries chromosomes alter and every living thing evolves into a new and varied species. However, what urged the chromosome to alter?

Mathematically and theoretically, it can be logically deduced that the original man in a hateful, wrathful, warrior rage, through his emotional intent, altered his binary DNA therefore his chromosomes ensuing his future path as a different coloured person.

Past life regressions have revealed that if you passionately detest another person from another race, you, over a period of life times, will physically alter to become that image. Through your emotional intent your binaries syncopated with your adversary's until you match perfectly. "Do unto others as it would be done unto you." The entire emotional journey was all about you.

My genetic line has a great grandfather, great grandmother, grandfather, father, mother, brother, sister aunts and uncles all average height six foot to six foot four. But right smack in the middle is my grandmother all four foot eleven of her. She had a violent fiery temper; she constantly displayed emotions of jealousy, envy, gluttony and covetness. She reacted badly to everything, like a spoilt brat.

Aesthetically and mathematically, this does not deduce. What caused the drastic alteration in the genetic line?

Through many years of hypnotherapy research, a group of us were able to unfold many different aspects of the Reincarnational Continuum or the cycle of how "History Repeats Itself."

What our research unveiled was that although our emotional reactions to various situations do determine our future paths, they also determine our physical appearance and just like the gaseous path, this emotional path is already predestined and out of our control.

The previous participants are already on the path. Your binaries and theirs already syncopate. You reacted, your egocentric survival instincts kicked in, altered your binaries and you joined them on that predetermined path, enhancing and upgrading your binaries, DNA and chromosomes, with each new existence.

What is in your control is your awareness to your instinctual reactions. They are what draws you into that oncoming traffic.

Due to centuries of inaccurate information, we have been reading our surroundings incorrectly, thus, creating more of the same karmic duality in timelines of ongoing injustice which we do not necessarily have to experience.

Our experiences are not necessarily the same path each time, however, the path is determined by a dominant faction of an emotional desire within you – hatred, anger, wrath, jealousy, fear, supremacy etc.-

The other revelation was that, although through karma, you may physically endanger another person's life, they will not in retribution be the ones to endanger your life in their next existence. Life is an ongoing continuum in forward motion, Fibonacci defines it cannot turn back on itself, however we do keep repeating the same scenarios over and over again simply using different emotional arenas.

The Karmic consequence is the result of each existence; however, you have a team of infiltrators following and leading you. The person in front of you, is the one you will endanger and the person following you will endanger you. Sarcastically putting it; this way everyone gets a turn to experience this emotional injustice utilising this particular emotion.

This is the ongoing forward motion of the continuum. This is the deciphering of the mirror forecast in Buddha teachings.

PAST AND FUTURE MIRROR EACH OTHER

YOU ECHO BOTH OF THEM; IN THE NOW.

By discovering through research, the speed with which the alteration of cells occurs and how every cell within our body alters at the same time instantly with the same force and impact, it helped us establish the swiftness within every immediate alteration that takes place throughout our bodies with our every thought, word and action.

Combining that information with our karmic information, it exposed how through the laws of duality, when struggling to lose weight, the focus is on trying to become healthy however, to understand the healthy person you must experience all that is dauntingly obese from every aspect, you now inadvertently are emotionally focusing on and empowering the fat person within you to not only put the weight back on but add extra pounds.

In an effort to embrace your healthier you, you have asked, therefore, empowering one emotion over the other. You have become victim to the emotional injustice of powerlessness.

Now you will experience this path from every emotional perspective, reacting to each one, then experiencing all the karmic repercussions thereof.

You will never understand the path of self-worth, until you experience worthlessness in its entirety.

Your path to healing is acknowledging that you and everybody in the entire world already are the embodiment of great health. You are wearing your body of history, so are they; along with all the repercussion to your past life emotional feelings of injustice. You are exactly as you should be, for a reason. You are perfect

When you understand that the victim you see in the mirror is displaying all the atrocities of injustice you have experienced for over 200000 years and that without one single component of them you would not understand your victimised state. You would not understand that, in order for you to no longer be victim you had to be exposed to your emotional obesity. You now understand all the components that being healthy isn't, which means you now understand what being healthy is.

You would not appreciate the freedom of your inner beauty if your obesity hadn't explained the injustice of the imprisonment of this malformation from every perspective. Now you are victim to neither.

The phenomenal obese person within you who bravely showed you your past path, is also displaying your miraculous bravery within you now. You have a choice; accept it and bravely forge forward or remain in victim mode and re-question.

The more emotional the reactions, the more passionate and powerful we feel.

The more passionate and emotional we feel, the more concise and accurate the alterations in our binary.

The more concise the alteration to the binary, the more immediate we alter our DNA and start creating a new environmentally productive chromosome.

A new evolutionary embodiment of that emotion begins to appear to produce your new path immediately.

This new emotion was instantaneously recorded in your DNA for you to repeat over and over again at the same time in each life with the opposite and same impact, exactly.

A simple example would be; you arrive at a shopping centre and as you walk into the shops you are vulgarly accosted, abused, denigrated and humiliated by a huge bully before you because you took his car park. You feel wretched. You instinctively react; you retaliate.

By retaliating you are mirroring your accuser. Or as we say in civvy street "you became as bad and abusive as him."

In your next life instead of being the victim of the abuse you will become the opposite; the perpetrator. Then with the exact same impact of bullying intimidation and aggression, you will project that feeling onto another person making them feel as wretched as you do now. These emotions are now recorded within your DNA and at the same age and time in your next life you will carry out these same aggressive actions.

In your past you may have been a farmer and the tractor driver placed the tractor where you needed to place the newly delivered hay, so you abused him. This is the emotional impact you are re-living now.

This is the inevitable timeline within all of us. The time of the debarkle in each life time has already been assessed by the ongoing historical wave. Your past life mirrors your future lives. That's your inevitable path and you keep re-living them over and over again.

Pending on the type of emotional reaction you implemented will determine from which perspective your next experience will be performed. From that moment on you start physically altering your appearance to become the embodiment of the emotions of the person who abused you.

They physically represented the embodiment of the emotional injustices displayed before you; anger rage aggression and victimisation. Now you will start changing your appearance to look like the same physical embodiment of those emotions.

We are billions of cells and each cell has a personality. When someone accosts you with hatred, all your binaries of those hatred cells match and combine to formulate a shape, a style, a personality. Your hair and skin start drying out, you get wrinkly and old, you get tired easily; you start physically wearing as your garment, all the traits of the emotion of hatred.

OR YOU COULD ALTER IT.

By responding, as opposed to reacting, you can recognise that all your past lives are being displayed before you and you are now re-living those experiences. In your past lives you have been both the aggressor and defender of this occurrence. It always took place at the same time, at the same age, with the same emotional impact in every existence. You are now re-living it again because you maintained it by reacting to it in your past. If you react again, you will return as the aggressor again in your next life.

You now understand that by not empowering this victimised state it has no future path. You can alter this entire debarkle.

Instead of adding fuel to the fire again, you can realise you already have all the justice you will ever need. This has already been taken care of. Quietly apologise out of respect, and move on realising and allowing all to be perfect.

This will alter not only your future but his future timelines as well. Next life time for both of you, when the time arrives, this incident will occur in a completely different more pleasant manner.

Then let it go. Do not concentrate on the incident in any way. To focus on any fraction of it is to empower that individual portion to maintain injustice. Refrain from feeling intimidated or victimised for if you do, this disturbance will also activate some injustice within you to experience in future timeline. The path of wretchedness because you are still dividing your feelings into victim and abuser mode again.

Now comprehend that in your past life at that same age and time you physically carried out the same actions to someone else and it was recorded in your genetic codes to recur over and over again. This person in front of you is only informing you of what you did. They are informing you of how you made the other person feel. However, now you are actually re-living this occurrence in your here and now. This is not some reincarnational act that took place somewhere in your past,

THIS WAS YOUR LIFE, NOW.

By realising that you now have neutralised the abuser and victim component within you as equal, you have refrained from giving either individual emotion power over the other. You have relinquished your inner emotional power struggle that takes place at that precise time of every existence. You have gained understanding and self-empowerment within you. You owe this fantastic transformation to the person in front of you, for without their service to you, your pastlife bravery would never have been divulged.

THIS IS JUSTICE

With this new attitude you have also altered your physical appearance to one of valour. No altercation of any kind will occur in your future for you have recorded harmony and courage within you genetic DNA code at this time in your future life. You have registered peace and balance within you. Now let the universe show you what you look like. You will from this moment on start genetically altering your physical appearance into that brave persona instantly.

When debarkles are constantly in front of you and you consistently react to them, as you age this information registers within your DNA, then starts your reincarnational path, altering your physical appearance through the aging process, illness and physical disabilities.

You start forgetting things; what you were previously thinking about; where you put things. Things that will no longer be required on your new path.

You start deleting your old programs within you and replacing them with the new upgrades for your new path.

You gain a limp; teeth need repair, hair thins out. Aches and pains appear that weren't there before. Age lines start appear on your face. Your body starts making you appear like a relative or the perpetrator who is your abuser; an alcoholic, an assailant, a drug addict. You start speaking like them, acting like them. You take on their personality. You start physically transforming into them.

Outsiders will comment how your child looks like more like you every day, however, again we are reading our feedback backwards. It is the other way around. You are following in their footsteps.

Our physical format is not the only way one suffers. Our environment takes a beating also. It too must adapt to concur with your binary.

Today we now ask why does Covit exists? It too was an evitable historical path created by humans with precise time lines. Cells within cells; same as what occurs within us, also physically performs in our outside world. This is also your feedback.

When the covit19 virus hit the world, no one stood up and took responsibility. They all blamed each other, for in truth with our vain perceptions of our own invincibility, to conceive that we could be responsible for such diabolical destruction would be ludicrous.

When I was a little girl, the town I lived in had a population of 76000 people. That message was on a sign on the outskirts of town that we passed every morning on our way to school.

The centre of town had the main square consisting of a Mother's war memorial, a huge department store, two banks and a chemist. This town was renowned for its fog, mist and rain. Many a tourist would jokingly claim, "Yes I passed through your town, but never saw it."

We celebrated the Carnival of Flowers, for due to the moisture and climate, the local's gardens excelled throughout the nation.

Our hottest day would have been in a very rare heat wave period where the temperature in February would have reached a scorching 29 degrees Celsius or 85 degrees Fahrenheit for about two days. On average, we would be inundated by three cyclones from around Australia day, January 26th to the end of February.

Winter was our purgatory as well as our redemption. My family lived on the outskirts of the town and we were nurtured in the hillside facing the eastern valley. The temperature there was always considerably warmer than the town. We would arrive at school in cooler clothing, completely unaware of the temperature difference, only to freeze for the day.

The centre of town was a vortex for the most insufferable blasting winter gales. We could stand on the any corner and the cold August winds would blow right through you, stifling all your bones to freezing point.

Annually we had the black frosts at the end of winter. These treacherous frosts devoured everything in their sight. They were so detrimental to the area nothing survived. They would spread across the entire Downs Region. Fruit orchids, crops, gardens, all wiped out with one frost bitten breath. The dew was like thick sheets of dry ice across the south eastern region of Queensland.

The frosts would last several days; then the sun would bleed through the cold air; the spring rains would trickle through and spring would bring forth the most amazing new life preparing the town for the onslaught of hay fever and our yearly carnival.

Crops across the region would flourish, giving birth to our wine and fruit orchids which were the best and sweetest in our state.

All the rats, mice, vermin, germs, infections, were annihilated and the dawn of the next season's profitable productivity exposed herself.

When I grew up, like all young people, I left the town for the city life, under some false pretence that life would be better. Employment was, for I never found it difficult to find work.

Then life bought me back home as it inevitably does and the township had developed and grown. I didn't think much of it at the time, but my little home town had expanded, developed, evolved.

I then married and travelled again and it wasn't for another twenty years that I would make my final return to the largest inland city in our state with an estimated population of 170,000.

The newly developed Downs Region was now suffering long enduring droughts and water shortages, intense bushfires, loss of farms and housing. However, due to the huge growth of suburbia and the clearing of the land, trees, bushes and the natural environment, my cool moist little home town was exchanged to a hotter, more artificial tar and cement civilised environment.

The town became a copycat of the big cities. Our parks became council orientated, not natural, with exercise gyms, and parks with tree bark as grass as oppose to real grass. All the tall shady eucalyptus and gum trees and natural life have been exchanged for asphalt and mortar, bridges, condos, motels shopping centres and very exclusive, expansive housing.

Single streets are now two, three and four lanes. Huge shopping malls in the inner city struggling to gain customer attention plus a minimum one major shopping centre at least at every town entrance from the country.

The temperature of the town has risen by at least 15 degrees. We were once renowned for several inches of rain per year, now we are very lucky to receive sufficient to fill our single dam and we live on extreme water restrictions.

We haven't seen a black frost for over six years and the cold winds of August are non-existent. We no longer receive the autumn, spring nor the winter rains. However, this year we reached the scorching temperature of over 42 degrees celsius in a heat wave and devastating fires that lasted over three months. Yet no one notices how much we've evolved.

This is the world of the next generation; they don't know who we were. They will know heat waves, climate change, and pandemics of infectious bacteria.

The invasion of covit19 has finally made her appearance known. Death-defying germs like hers have always been around, but we were simply able to contain her with our climate. Now with climate change, the entire world has allowed and adapted a new environment for her to exist in.

These forms of viruses were always around. However, this is evolution in the making and the civilised educated white narcissistic Adam created it by empowering the unnatural environment that contained her. However, the civilised human refuses to acknowledge the onus on his shoulders for the part he played in this controversy.

HE WAS WARNED!

The Aboriginals and Indians didn't understand Darwin's theories or his science, but they understood nature and its balance. They understood the neutrality of the balance. They understood that by dividing the environment and empowering one section over another creates imbalance and horrendous repercussions.

They have continuously warned the educated white Adam and Eve not to destroy the oasis's. They warned them that the balance of nature is vital to the ongoing survival of man and all species; but did they listen? NO! "We are British. We are Spanish. We are European. We are American. We are Christians. We are civilised. We are educated. You are heathens and barbarians and uneducated monkey men."

The educated civilised white ADAM bought with them to Australia and other nations, disease and more white humans under penitentiary conditions. They encroached the bays of the oasis in both America and Australia. They trespassed inland stripping the oasis even further. They obliterated the protection and production of all the native wildlife, for they deemed them all as pests, obstructions to civilised progress.

These civilised nationals then introduced to the small oasis, obese livestock and farm animals; but the oasis could not sustain such beasts. So, the educated humans stripped the oasis even further to introduced farms for their fodder, for their newly introduced beasts of burden, cattle, sheep, horses, camels, pigs and chickens. They culled and slew all native animals for they were a threat to this newly introduce breed of stock and their food production.

Being labelled as pests the native animals were ousted and now had no homes, no food, no protection. They had to be eliminated and one by one many were exterminated culled and made extinct. This practice continues today. The amazing Australian tradition of the culling of the roos or dingos.

In Northern New South Wales, the Northern hairy nosed Wombat population of over 40,000 was culled to extinction. In South Eastern Queensland they are still the seventh most endangered species in the world, if not taken care of carefully they could be extinct in the short-term. The

300 or so that still exist are protected on small reserves. In drought season their food and water is subsidised, but that still may not be enough.

However, in NSW the civilised educated farmers needed the water from the oasis for their fodder, so these native animals were deemed as pests, like rabbits.

The farmers built dams, pipelines, any means necessary to extract the water from the natural oasis to ensure the ongoing productivity of the introduced beasts, wheat, fodder and cotton, at the cost of all native and natural life downstream.

They introduced chemicals and insecticides to protect their invaluable crops, disintegrating all the water ways with toxic waste and poisons. This then depleted stocks of all the natural life forms of the Murray-Darling dependent on the water including our infamous Murray Cod.

They then proceeded to turn the rich healthy element of this country that had not seen disease or poverty for over 20000 years into their diseased ridden, drought stricken, struggling civilisation, just like their prehistoric civilised empires of Europe and Britain they abandoned and left behind. Why did they come here in the first place?

History repeating itself; their countries could no longer sustain the humans in their own environment. These criminals were the starving and the destitute. They were so poor they were stealing food to survive. They were convicted and sent to the colonies thousands of miles from their families loved ones and homes never to see them again.

This Adam and Eve Empire was the civilised national representation of Britain that had the audacity to steal from innocent natives and trespass on their nation, because "they were civilised and more educated."

Just like their religions and history, all of our Australian history is portrayed from the white British man's perspective. The white man transcribes how harsh the land is to the Australian farmers; how difficult it has been for two maybe three generations of family farmers who have supported the white man's pompous lifestyle of settlements ruled by British governments filled with greed and gluttony for over two hundred years.

Many of our country and western folk singers pour out their bleeding hearts of the difficulties of the struggle the white man has had to endure. Hit country song after hit song of desperate struggles, generation after generation for two hundred years, but none have asked the first nation owners how they feel. How after 20000 years of disease-free equal existence in peace and harmony with all life forms, they are now deemed to whiteman's hell of imbalanced incarceration.

No one has asked them to tell their story. No one asked them how they felt when this tyrannical group of diseased ridden white caucasian barbarians invaded their peaceful country and through violence, and the introduction of guns and warfare stole their country and all its natural resources from them for their productivity and profitability; then proceeded to destroy it, by degrees, under the name of …., actually, there is no name for legal dereliction and usurping.

Like the native animals, the original owners were ousted from their land, their homes like pests for over one hundred and fifty years and now they have to, by cultured law, sit back and watch, while these book-educated barbaric front-runners destroy their very livelihood and them as well. The livelihood they protected and nurtured for over 20000 years.

Our First Owners tended this land for centuries successfully, productively and without disease. It took the civilised educated Christian orientated British white Adam and Eve less than 200 years to infect and kill all the water, earth, land and natural resources, almost to extinction.

It took the Americans less than three hundred years to achieve the same horrendous decimation, but America is bigger. However, the pattern and life sentences for both denigrating specimens, are the same. Are they going to recognise or render their mistakes? No. It's now climate change. It's out of their hands.

The problem belongs to something or someone else. They are civilised, they are educated. They are above such menial tasks. They are the supreme sons of Adam and Eve

Exposed in front of us on a daily basis, is visual analysis of how all our binaries are integrated as feedback. How we work as emotional humans and how our evolution works. It is not the strongest shall survive, for we are immortal we all will survive, it is how we will survive, that is our dilemma.

We are being shown the information that the natives in America and Australia all understood centuries ago. They understood that through actions and reactions, all things alter and those reactions alter all life forms in existence instantly.

The ongoing emotional injustices of Adam and Eve within us personally alter our chromosomes in exactly the same way as nature echoed her response to the white man. Evolution doesn't happen to us, we create it.

The First National Owners of America, Northern Europe, Australia, Incas, and Aztec, understood this. They comprehended this, however, because they didn't attend a stonework artificial church or temple and they interpreted the cosmic force through their environment, they were classed as uneducated philistines.

The matrix binary of mother nature matched theirs and they listened; but according to the supreme civilised Christians they were in cahoots with some devil so they were classified as lower class, ignoramuses.

The natives listened to the binaries of the animals, the wind, the clouds. They could read the alterations in their environment and climate. If animals departed or arrived, the matrix binary was upgrading and altering. This meant, expect a sudden change in the weather patterns.

If the black cockatoo, willy wag tail or currawong showed up, floods and destruction or dry weather would be predicted. Centuries of practical knowledge handed down from generation to generation to maintain the protection and production of ALL species equally. Everything was in balance.

If clouds were sleek and smooth, huge thunder storms were predicted. They didn't need the confines of cement block church to inform them that mother nature had a cyclone preparing her way to give them the water they needed for the next season, so, batten down the hatches.

Adam's white man's ministry had some old eccentric donned in church finery stand in front of his racist congregation and preach the fine art of dictatorship.

He preached how to be bigoted, prejudiced old men, supreme to all the beings and natives as well all-natural life.

He dictated his dominance as white man. He preached Adam and Eve's duality on how to empower the emotional art of injustice over another. He taught them how to divide your house into many variants of different prejudiced emotions then enforce them on your brother.

He had neither the intelligence nor the brainpower to know that in doing so he would re-live a timeline of an ongoing onslaughts of injustice of the same actions and reactions for centuries to come. He also, had no idea of balance and oneness or how to save his congregation from a flood or drought.

The native's divinity spoke to them directly of the sanctity of all life in unison with all things and it still does. But these uncultured swine needed to be civilised and educated.

The high-handed Christian Church elders dictated that these pagans, as in children, for their own safety, be abducted and taken from their loved ones and families and force fed the Adam and Eve's civilised bullshit of narcissistic male dominance.

They literally re-lived their past history by enslaving these children and forcing them to rebuild their empire again. Same timeline, same rules and laws as imposed throughout Europe and England during the middle ages only a different country. Child labour at no cost to any empires. This time the innocent children were forced to build the outback.

The Judean/Latin Roman God perceived by white men will never save Adam and Eve' arse. This God will never redeem these white men. They will however experience their hell; for it was through this blackmailing myth of terror that the children were co-erced to slave labour.

These holier than thou "Profanity of God" may inform themselves that they, because they were appeasing their God, will experience a happier and healthier place, but their threats will transform them into the very devils they feared and grant them their future perdition they have re-created for them to experience. By voicing their hell, they are verbally deeming their future path and this will be the educated Adam and Eve's future diabolical path.

The unravelling of this earthly hell will determine how it all balances out; how this will all end. All Gods were created from man's perception 200000 years ago. Compare the perception of a God created two hundred thousand years ago by the generation of heavy-handed Adam and Eves to the native God of the aboriginals and natives who listened to nature and allowed for over 200000 years.

Adam and Eve will never take responsibility for their actions and will call on their heavenly perception of their God on his puffed-up cloud to continue to help them. So, this hellish exhumation of mankind will continue as the educated white man again turns a blind eye over and over again to his irresponsibility.

To appease their economical money Gods, the national supervisors will open its doors to more international occupancy. To allow more occupancy they need to eradicate more of the sacred life-giving oasis and expand into it with more artificial means of support.

They will build more of their artificial paradise with asphalt, tar, cement, bridges, roadways, housing, shopping centres, schools, gymnasiums, motels, hotels, sports centres, hospitals, social centres, expanding, developing, erasing, increasing, and enlarging.

Next step, because we as a nation can no longer support our own country with the fundamental food resources like our civilised predecessors, we will have to import them. We will support our cheaper less costly neighbours. They do not have the same hygienic principles as we do for, they raise their stock and vegetables based on their ethnic values introducing new types of unsafe diseases to us through their food. This theory has already been proven before, however this is a new generation; desperate times, desperate measures.

Our climate alterations will continue to rise to extremes and become worse, thus creating more fires, droughts, and starvation of animals and beasts. More adaptable environments for further undesirable diseases to exist until the viruses overtake the world in plague proportion and finally man in human form shall become extinct, due to some invisible bug created by white educated man because he neglected to balance his environment.

Then little by little because the viruses no longer have a vehicle to sustain them; they too will become extinct.

Mother nature won't waste any time rebalancing and destroying all evidence of the human's existence. She will, just as they did, exterminate them from actuality. The tar, asphalt and chemical cement will be expunged from existence. All the bridgeways, roadways highways, and suburbs will collapse back into the natural soil again, only now the soil will be morphed with the new toxic chemicals from the buildings, bridges, asbestos, metals and cement.

The waterways will become riddled with poisonous toxic waste, however, like the virus, a new breed of life will evolve from this new environment. Nature herself will have created the new chromosomes for the future existence of these new unknown species. Balance, unlike this one, but balance just the same, will be restored after two maybe three thousand years.

This is the ongoing timeline of the Reincarnational Continuum or History Repeating Itself. After the asteroid dissemination that covered the world with radiation and created the ice age, it started to melt; and from the waters a new world regrouped and man as Neanderthal and Mediterranean hairless white nation emerged.

Mother Nature doesn't need you; you are nothing more than an intricate cell. She will survive without you. She has done it before millions of times and she will do it again. Mother Earth does not need you but, you do need Mother Nature.

When you look at a tree you see branches, trunks and leaves.

When you look at the ocean you see water for miles and miles.

When you look at the mountains, valleys and vistas you see panoramic views.

When you look at a human you see the human form.

Every single one of them is created under the same format. The truth is, the humans, the mountains, the oceans, the vistas do not exist as such. What does exist is the miniscule cell within every cell that contains all the information of the universe past, present and inevitable futures and *it* embodies all living things.

Innumerable amounts of individual cells, all reacting and acting in the same manner, attracting and repelling, creating dynamic structures for you to breeze across, forming magnificent wonders before your eyes, and you have no idea that they exist, because you don't see them.

The Adam and Eve instinct have and always will treat all other beings in existence with despotism, because it has an ego instinct that defines itself as supreme. This psyche judges all things through us from this victimisation emoted perspective of survival and it has bought us to this point.

It still assumes itself to be of a Godhead. It still believes itself to be invincible. It has survived through false perceptions of its supremacy verses inferiority for centuries and constantly refuses to acknowledge that its enemy is simply the mirror image of itself being exposed to him in that time and at that moment.

Our original binary of Adam and Eve remains steadfast in its right to survive. It refuses to acknowledge its continued path of injustice. It refuses to understand that you need both together to truly survive. He sees it all as weaknesses; as a result, we all keep re-creating our ongoing timelines of the duality riddled with these karmic imbalances.

With every opinion we share, we are voicing our Godhead supremacy. Without knowing it we automatically assume supremacy over others thus create another emotional reaction defining their inferiority within them; but they are not inferior, they are the opposite side of us but of equal value.

Every thought word or action we carryout, be it anger, greed, envy, pride, wrath gluttony, lust, sloth, we intertwine them with our feeling of injustice, then experience the inequality, victimisation through this new emotion. Every time we react to a new emotion, we upgrade our injustice with this new emotion then we have to re-experience the entire debarkle again with all the new added karmic responses.

We have to experience all there is to know about injustice,
inequality, victimisation and powerlessness;
To understand the gift of justice, equality, self-empowerment and self-love,

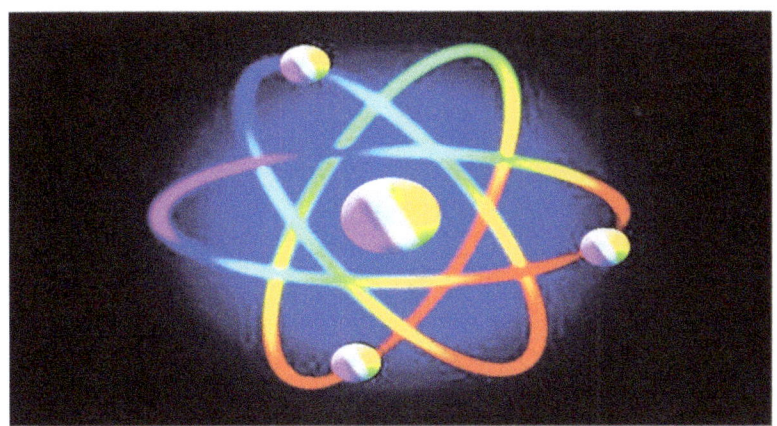

I WAS EVOLUTION

NOW CAN YOU SEE ME?

Chapter Four

I Am Inequality

NOW SEE ME

We as a human race have been taught that we exist in a universe of karmic duality. For every inequality there is an equality of the same value. If you are genuinely seeking true equality then you will experience inequality from every emotion of injustice available to mankind for thousands of centuries.

For you to appreciate true equality and freedom you have to experience the imprisonment and discrimination of inequality and powerlessness to the same and equal impact that you desire it. This is Karma.

When you are experiencing any form of discontent, within you, there is also an emotion of content equivalent in value in your inevitable future waiting for you to allow.

We are the embodiment of our continued injustice; predator verses victim, inequality. Our entire world divulges this information to us from every perspective. By reacting to any injustices, the new emotions transform our physical body and we commence our new incarnation as that new emotional judgement.

By focusing on the inequality of the new singular emotion, you are able to intensify that specific feeling, opening it up to more amplified malcontent. Then by reacting to that experience again from a different emotional perspective you upgrade that experience and re-live it all again and so you keep going on and on.

It is only when you reach the point of realisation that you understand the futility of the ongoing exercise. You then assess that, without that entire horrendous experience, without every detailed incident, you would not be at your point of realisation today. You wouldn't understand your ongoing continuum of victimisation.

Realisation alters the entire equation. Your perspective alters, your attitude alters, your outside world alters, your physical appearance alters.

Now you understand you already have everything you need within you. You understand that instead of chasing it, fighting for it and trying to achieve and control it thus becoming its ongoing victim; you allow it. You allow it in all its entirety to come to you and magically display itself in front of you through a friend's complaints of their struggling life.

You too are allowed to join in the vicitmising session, or, you can appreciate your friend and the miraculous circumstances you are re-experiencing with them. You can generate all the new magical abundance of true equality into both your lives without question.

For you to appreciate equality you must experience inequality.

For you to appreciate justice you must first experience injustice

For you to appreciate true bravery and strength you must experience powerlessness and fear.

For you to appreciate love, abundance and happiness, unfortunately you must have experienced loneliness, hatred, poverty, isolation impoverishment and despair.

All perceptions of your emotions are within you at all times. It's your focused attention on one over the other that divides them and you. You then empower that individual emotion and see your outer world in disrepute from that perspective.

You see the world as ugly and painful, unjust and cruel. You judge or analysis your situation from your supercilious Adam and Eve instinct. You then receive more of the same, because you are your supercilious ego and you can only live all your existences from his attitude. You think what you seeing is a fact outside of you, un- attached, but it is all you. It is all your unseen matrix binaries in action.

If you learn to allow your Eve with your Adam. You will evolve into a new species. You will see your world from a more empowering light and your outer world will alter to this new balanced perspective. The divided world around you of Adam verses Eve will become powerless.

Karmic duality exists because you believe you are divided. This is the path of the defensive survival, instinct; you have to dominate and win, or submit and lose; this is the divided path displayed by Adam and Eve. You will experience all the paths of injustice from their perception. This emotion can create these existences through murder, wars, and impoverishment.

You do not understand the majesty of a full cup, until you experience the void when it is empty.

Don't go looking for something because when you do you reignite the lack victim within you again. You do not believe you have already received all of it. Therefore, you start questioning from this need, separation, impatience and want. You are again empowering an emotion of victimisation, and will walk that path until it is done. Why settle for a paper cup when the universe wants to supply you with your own ocean, river, stream, creek and spring.

You may be experiencing wretchedness; it is that emotional injustice that is determining your future paths through victimisation. It has you imprisoned, but you don't have to be.

After 200000 years we have never had this opportunity before. We now know how to alter our attitudes to give us paths of exhilaration and joy. This is now a choice we've never had before. Which path do we want to choose? Ongoing victimisation and wretchedness, or your already predetermined path of freedom, abundance and happiness.

We cannot alter what has happened, we should not want to, for everything is perfect and without any component of your past you would not have reached this realisation, but now we can alter our reactions to them and alter our future outcomes.

The inevitable facts of the Milky Way and the collision with Andromeda are predetermined and out of our hands.

Earth is already destined to this path of destruction. This is the ways of evolution but, if you have the impudence to still believe you will be exiting on earth in four billion years, then I strongly recommend you close this book now for the future information I'm about to disclose to you will literally break your heart.

Similar to the crossword, the destiny of the Milky Way is pre-ordained to change. That is inevitable. That we cannot alter.

What is important and necessary now is, what we can alter. How are we going to alter our future paths which have been scholastically determined by our civilised educated Adam and Eve over their descendants, when those declarations have been treacherously incorrect for centuries.

There are many impossible alternatives but due to Adam and Eve dominance they are doomed to failure.

If the born natives of both countries America and Australia were in the position to retrieve any of the property seized by the white man; and then, if they were to restore that land back to its natural resources; would that make a difference?

No. Previous historical timelines have displayed deliberate patterns portrayed by these educated civilised white supremists before. The narcissistic species persists on winning, at any cost. History concludes one of two things would then definitely prevail.

In Australia the mentality of Anglo-Saxon governments would ordain that they reclaim the land under some governmental restricted back law dating back two centuries, not for justice, but for greed and avarice then retrieve their land for more expansion and do it all again for the profitability and western capitalism

Or two, the superiors would claim total responsibility for the renovations and banish the natives off the land again, then proceed to destroy it utilising their old uneducated productivity procedures which were incapable of sustaining their life in the first place. So, they will again eradicate all-natural life forms that obstruct them and recreate the more imbalances; that's all they know.

FACT: In central Australia an aboriginal clan regained their land and were achieving wonderous independence results their way and in their own right.

A newly elected Australian govt instigated a new control board for some bullshit reason, now these government bureaucrats are lining their pockets with the funds deemed for the enrichment of the aboriginal clan and the aboriginals are again fighting for their rights. The aboriginals are back struggling and starving again. They under this new regime will never redeem their land again nor their independence.

The path of inequality displayed daily throughout Australian history under any white Leadership, is exposed through many varied and different emotions. The aboriginals have never gained or been treated with any respect they deserve nor will they ever. Although this is an ongoing timeline, of powerlessness, it still does not condone the actions of any corporate government.

Respect of course would be the ultimate option. It would truly render all the damage done over the past two to three centuries, but it is an unrealistic, untouchable unfathomable dream and will never happen under any white government regime.

For us to understand equality we have to experience inequality at its worst. Our aboriginals are our teachers. The condescending attitude of our governments force the ongoing difficulty. Our aboriginals have immeasurable difficulty being educated under white man's supremist tutorials. This patronising educational system prevents the aboriginals from even desiring to go to white man's university. What's the use?

The use is the importance of recognising that the knowledge of the first owners is irreplaceable. Recognising that ALL-natural life is important and plays an integral role in our future survival, plus appreciation that the oasis is invaluable to our nation and so are the original owners.

The inequality and injustice against our first owners are still appalling by human rights standards and our governments constantly turn a blind eye because the dominant Adam ethos dictates this race to be of lessor value, uneducated heathens and they, the white man, they are the highly educated and civilised race.

Our Adam orientated governments are writhing with socialistic lawyers, qualified business men, educated in prominent British orientated schools and universities. They are urbane white Adam's who are taught the lurks and perks of being underhandedly smarter than the average bear.

They discuss *peace, by means of war and destruction,* at international conferences but in truth they have no idea how to accomplish it.

They deliberately lie and swindle each other to manipulate other country's resources to maintain financial prosperity for themselves and their position on the international markets, while the very essence of the countries they represent are in ruin and slowly dying.

Yet, we have to support them, for to ignore this floor show of educated propensity would be suicide as a nation and we could not exist on the fluctuating world markets.

What if we gave our next generation another option? What if as part of their school curriculum we taught them the truth from all perspectives? Gave them back their dignity.

What if the history taught to our nations was the true history of our nations, not some a one-sided version to purvey the white hedonistic supremacy of Adam and the British empire as taught by old men centuries ago? Old men who wrote the books filled with prejudices and racism of all nations propelling them against each other?

What if our songs and anthems told the truth about the unfairness against all the native and secular groups, animals and land? What if our future path was one where the next generation didn't see mixed races. A generation who were able to reach out together as one populace to create reformation for a more balanced world wise future?

This could be our KEY. The narcissistic male supremist from over 200000 years ago maintained control through fear violence and separation, by refraining from allowing *all peoples to be treated equally.* They are not more educated or smarter or more intelligent. They simply used their arrogant bullying tactics to determine the rules and control the people.

These are exciting times. For the first time in over 20000 centuries, women and ethnic groups not only are allowed to be educated; they are allowed to advance their education to the betterment of themselves, their family, industry, their country and their future.

This was our first step to freedom; our first glimpse at true equality and independence. However, that is only the first step. We are still being taught the old narcissistic doctrinated principles.

This was why we never fought back. We were never allowed to be educated. If we questioned authority including our husbands, we'd be physically throttled. For if a woman were to be educated, yes, we would question authority; and yes, we would more than likely undermine authority and that could never have been not allowed.

We experienced inequality at its worst. If we fought back, we would have lost. Now we have discovered that by understanding those ruthless acts of barbarism we can use that knowledge as the tools we need to empower us. Without them in my past, I could never have reached this state of realisation that the actions of the past are not the path to equality, in my here and now.

Our fight was not simply the discrimination against women it is the narrow-mindedness against mankind in general. Even today our narcissistic Australian government departments and the American governments are ignoring the radicalisms and deaths of their negros and our aboriginals in custody. *"It's not their problem."*

These are the lying garments your political faction's wear. It exposes them for autocrats they really are. These people are the leaders you elected, because you knew no better. However, through intense adversity some female leaders have stepped up and demonstrated empowering strength and clarity and resolve under the harshest of conditions with peace and dignity.

Queensland Premier Anastacia Palaszczuk and Jacinta Adhern NZ Prime Minister both stood up against horrendous narcissistic odds during the Covit pandemic and won. Not just won; THEY WON, empowering women everywhere.

Of a morning I drive down my street to my store. My little town has grown. She is now more multi- cultural and the segregation is more obvious than before with all inter-racial breeds vying for their position in the pecking order. The Asians and white caucasian are exposing their supremacy by being driven to their private Christian schools in their upmarket cars, while a group of beautiful aborigines walk on the footpath opposite this prestigious future generation to the state school up the road.

The opportunities for the private school students in the future will be optimal due to their parent's money and influence and that is fine. The opportunities for these state school students will be minimal due to their lack of funds. If we were to balance or equalise this act, based on previous historical timelines, this *is* what would happen.

In the 1990's when the AIDS pandemic was at its highest in plague proportion, a vaccine was formulated and made available to the American public for $15000p/a due to the pharmaceutical company investors dire need to cash in on the pandemic and redeem a huge profit. This is the egocentric psyche of Adam as the leader of the world, with power and greed. This is what he had to do in the past to survive and win. This is our evolutionary path to the westernised privatisation and capitalism.

With the assistance of *the inventors of Doctors Without Borders* a manufactured generic brand of the same vaccine was made available in south east Asia for the high-risk victims in the third world countries for $1 per day. Ratio wise this was the third world equivalent to the world market price.

The privileged sector of the American society did their homework and discovered the price differentiation and demanded the same *equal rights* for all Americans thus, forcing their government to supplement the western pharmaceutical companies billions of dollars making the vaccine available to all Americans at a similar price as the third world countries.

Because the Bush government coped the phenomenal pharmaceutical bill, the American government and marketing establishments started a reprehensible slur campaign against the East Asian pharmaceutical company denigrating and defaming them and their work, stating their laboratory conditions were that of third world country standards, rat hoarders and declared them unsafe, unsound and unhealthy.

All contracts with this pharmaceutical company, which had supported America civilisation for decades with generic brands, were now severed. The civilised materialistic American Government rebuked another country because they saw a means to assist a third world country against another world virus instigated through the white man diseases.

With this same knowledge, if we were to allow a financial system in our society where we could educate the aborigines to a higher standard, where *their* principles, ethics, values and morals could be taught with a higher more dignified environmental outcome.

If we could provide them with their own university courses where they and all others could study their own laws as well as international laws and create their own politicians who could stand beside all the narcissistic socialists to render a plan to save the earth by teaching them how to replace tar and cement with a more environmentally safe prognosis.

If we gave them the opportunity to stand tall instead of being deliberately quashed and made invisible, by the dictatorial educated white Adam, do you believe for one minute it would be allowed?

As a nation; as a country; as a world, do you believe for one minute the white democratic civilised society of Adam and Eve would allow it to prevail, when they would have to still pay for their own university education. When it is their 5-billion-dollar prestigious apartments with the boat moorings on the waterfronts that may be in jeopardy?

Dream on.

In one of Gardener Laurence's books regarding the myths of the ark of the covenant, he determines that the arc was actually a solar battery-operated electric rod created thousands of years ago in Egyptian times. It had the capability of turning specific soil into a form of liquid gold. Liquid gold was then deemed the "manna from heaven."

If you were ill, it had the capability of altering all your DNA generic codes and you were completely healed of all ailments.

In chapter eleven of his book, an American lived on a farm with soil that was useless. He sent it for analysis and an excited European group of scientists returned and experimented on this soil with exceptional success.

They placed it under extensive heat for longer periods than usual and the results were more productive than they expected. They decided to market their new product as an anti-cancer drug.

But in truth, it was miraculous. Needless to say, what the underhanded pharmaceutical and governing agents did to his company, his home, and his family was not only unacceptable but utterly soul-destroying. They sabotaged and burnt his business and classed it as nuclear waste, destroyed his home and land, his family, his health, and his life, libelling him as a fraud.

The truth is; if he was a fraud, they would not have taken so much trouble to destroy him and they would not have worried about him.

He found something and they had to destroy him before he destroyed them. It was another greedy instinctual survival tactic.

However, in South East Queensland, unbeknownst to financial pharmaceutical hierarchy, about a decade ago, there was a small no name doctor who did the same thing.

He didn't advertise his cures. He quietly proceeded to heal all his terminally ill orientated patients who were sent to him through word of mouth.

Those who didn't believe his healing works called him a fraud for if it truly worked, he would advertise it. He knew better. He passed recently and his recipe supposedly went with him.

This unfortunately is our actuality of our reality.

> It is incredibly sad to have to come to terms with the
> reality of our civilised materialistic society.

There are permanent cures for all things, but you will never receive them for there is no money in that. There could be peace but there is no money in that.

In the sixties, we walked, we protested, we stood up, and for a short term, our peers saw us. Our songs, the poems, the protests of the sixties don a period where voices were being heard.

The young leaders were listening. Leaders who were standing with the people. Changes were being made. The new invigorating leaders were young and saw a future of hope. They allowed education for everyone in schools. They started treating all our young generation as equal regardless of colour, creed, gender or value.

They were eradicating bigotry, sexism, racism and war. They were creating a united front and a united world. They were standing with us and forging us all forward as one with exciting futures.

We had them for almost a decade. 1960-1968. Then one by one every single one of these dynamic leaders were assassinated by bullets and replaced with the old archaic principles of Adam again. Leaders who again manipulated us and returned us to the worldly cycle of tumultuous competitiveness, survival and warfare. All our spontaneous work, our enthusiasm and excitement were torn apart and scrapped.

The protesters were all thrown in front of the new army tanks to perish. Had this happened before? Yes, same historical timeline, thousands of times, but this time instead of it being Lincoln, it was Kennedy.

All our progress was desecrated by the new egocentric Adam's political front. He as the new supremist leader blackmailed Australians back into the Vietnam war with his financial cronies creating one of the longest profitable futile wars of the century. Our reward was, Pizza Hut, Kentucky Fried, Macdonald's, American junk food merchandise and his duplicitous handshake.

Conspiracy or not, the six high-ranking American and international banks profited extremely well during that period, supporting both sides of the wars. It was strictly good business.

This has always been the case. Wars bring big money. When I was young one of the most horrendous rumours that shocked me was, that a profitable western country supplied the gas for the extermination of the Jews in Germany. It was simply good business.

For every yin there is a yang. To experience the marvels of peace; you must unfortunately experience all the desecrations of all hostilities through country, business and family.

However, what was also displayed in the sixties was that if we placed our future paths into the hands of a younger more dedicated generation, the journey to equality is not only possible but extremely probable. However, that gaseous path has already been paved now and through correct and honest education for all equally, the young may choose to take it.

To achieve that, we have to realise everyone and everything in the entire world, through our paths of abusive cantankerous inequality, has already achieved our existing path of equality and peace.

Now we have to walk it, live it

I WAS INEQUALITY

NOW CAN YOU SEE ME?

Chapter Five

I AM DIVIDED

NOW SEE ME

Upon departing the hospital, I was in the elevator when a stranger entered and stood near the door. Little did he know, he was about to be my inspiration. He was my Henri de Toulouse-Lautrec the 19th century post-Impressionist painter. His story narrates as him being a highly disabled cripple; he is also the renowned artist for the can-can series of art in Paris.

The story I was told was; he loved one woman only and he told her that he made a deal with his gods. He would suffer all the indignities of the world as a cripple so long as she would never have to suffer or bear any offensive pain or ugliness. He would also carry her share of any burden for he loved her so much and that this price was an honour in return for her love. She invariably gave it all to him without question.

In the elevator, the tall man stood before me. He was a victim of a horrendous accident. He was literally divided. His face was half missing, he had one ear missing ear, his arm had been severely burnt and he was missing some fingers and toes.

He stood before me and I could see him; clearly, from the outside and the inside.

This beautiful man was now visible everywhere he went, and his body was saying out loud, "now you see me. I reflect you. I know who I am. I'm better; stronger, than I ever was. I am not victim and have a happy life, for I now know how to have it all and I'm no longer invisible to anyone; you can see me and you cannot ignore me, but can you see you?

You are my outer reflection; how does that make you feel? Are you repulse, afraid, indignant? Can you see the real me? If you can then you can see the real you.

I stood before him; he didn't see me. I write books, I speak out, yet, no one sees or hears me. He stood before me and his body language was basically saying to me, "BE SEEN." Try harder.

It was through his extreme disability that he was now seen.
It was through his extreme disability that I could now see me.

He stood with me sharing an elevator. All I could feel was a strange peace. I didn't react to him. I have lived this path both before and now, only I was the victim. Maybe not burnt but seriously disabled, extremely divided.

He was also informing me that I would be seen, so be prepared to step up and be heard. This is you; you are me; now we are one together; be the best of both of us and speak for all of us.

He displayed horrific burns and debilities, yet he stood before me strong and courageous. He let me see that through all forms of maladies we find inner strength. Through powerlessness; we find true self-empowerment.

To appreciate true health, we must first experience all the components of detrimental illness, and these are vast and varied. From mental health to complete incapacitation.

The irony of all this was, I later recollected just how I would abhorrently judge the ugly puritanical white supremist Adam and Eve who detrimentally life after life defiled my every existence as both male and female. Here he was again, half damaged, half perfect, and he was informing me of who I was.

This man was wearing our division, informing me of how divided we are. Yet, as one we are unbelievably brave and can overcome all illness; By being one we allow our inner health.

> I have always been healthy; I simply have to allow it.

> By indicating I am healed I am also indicating I am unwell. I have to allow all "my healthy."

Poetically I had to blend my black with my white, my pink with my green, my blue with my orange my indigo with my yellow and empower all my colours equally to create my perfect rainbow of amazing human health within me; then live it.

I have a friend who informed me "I'm sorry darling, this world is not perfect." She has travelled the world, worked in Kuwait and experienced horrendous situations through the impoverishment of war and disease as a nurse. I know that she exists because I exist and I exist because she exists.

If any component of her life didn't occur exactly the way that it did, she would not be in my life for me to see how marvellous she really is. I needed to see that. For in seeing her antagonism I found my realisation. I cannot exist without her for she mirrors my karmic equal and opposite.

In her world of ongoing endless maladies, I am able to understand absolute perfection because her path was my path; is my path. I have also experienced every component of her path that's what she is explaining to me; so, today I can choose to continue or choose to no longer be victim.

The narcissistic ego of my supercilious Adam and Eve has always relayed him as the crème del la crème, and her as his enabler, when in truth his appearance is that of cold death walking. Both genders have to embellish, emboss, glitter up and substitute their human form for better, for centuries.

Frilled shirts, crinolines, pompadour wigs for both male and female. Breasts puffed up to sit on top of dresses, and men floating on ships with over rated gathered sleeved shirts with enough material to manufacture a wardrobe for an entire local native tribe.

Uniforms with gold tassels, and medals to prove their worth. This imitation of life described their pompous ass civility while they constantly destroyed all other innocent nations.

The American Civil War, the Napoleonic Wars, the Crusades, The Hundred Years wars, pretty grey clothes verse pretty blue clothes, but warfare, none the less. Billions upon billon of dollars spent on essential pretties to justify the reason why the educated man has the right to kill the uneducated man with lethal weapons. 200000 years and this is still their solution to life; kill or be killed.

"The survival of the fittest."

I sit in my coffee shops and I watch many a white Adam and Eve pass and they exude this blue-grey haze around them. They are old, wrinkled and frumpy or young and uncouth and frumpy. Even when dressed up, they lack that savior-faire. We have to procure medical procedures on all parts of our body to even be acceptable in our society today.

Make up has to cover up, lift, highlight, enlarge, shrink and that's just the face. Then there is the body.

The ongoing onslaught of adjustments, implants, to make us more visible to the real world as something else. Adjustments to our outer world to fabricate the white female form to look like the fictitious Viking Aaryan boy as dogmatically doctrinated in WW2 by Hitler.

The perfect specimen he called it; the putative Nordic or Aryan races of pure white skinned, blue eyes, blonde hair, and they have to look the same from the back as they do from the front. The young boys, skinnier the better; the men built like massive titans of muscles, but both are formed with the same fascist Adam supremist barbarianism.

This fictitious white dominant authoritarian force has expunged, exploited, denigrated and slandered all other breeds as lessor beings than he, as a means of his supreme survival instinct.

However, all the various coloured races display absolute beauty in all its forms from within; be they fat, thin, young or old. The first thing seen in the child is their eyes and their skin. They are always fresh, alive and sparkling. Then as they grow, they emanate a sensual beauty.

Lips so full, soft and succulent they could kiss you into the next century. Eyes that lure you into sensual ecstasy and make you smile.

Hair? Their beautiful dark or curly it is colourful, shiny, long and always lustrous and thick.

Their bodies. They have naturally beautiful full voluptuous bodies tall or short with curves and rolls and they explode with sensual prowess from every molecule in their physique.

Dance; my lord can they dance? From Polynesian islander throughout the world to Asian Indians to American Indians to Aborigines.

Sing? What they do to the blues, jazz, country and folk music makes the birds want to sing in harmony. Their voices can vibrate the very essence of your soul. When they sing in church choirs you either end up clapping or dancing or praising their lord even when you are non- believer.

The white bigots of Adam are the first to condemn any other race for their colour, ethical beliefs, talents and values. They are the first to condemn other lifestyles and they are the first to judge from their godhead superciliousness. "*They are not like us,*" unquote.

From my own personal Adam and Eve of my past, analysing from the white supremist bigoted perspective; if any God, anywhere, is the image of these racist supremists and has the nerve to deem me and other intergender as unworthy abominations; he is an ugly son of a bitch who needs to take a good look in a mirror.

As my *educated* hairdresser friends says; "*he ought to put mirror beside his bed and wake up to himself.*"

Their questionable doctrines constantly enforce ongoing narcissistic division in your inner house. "Love your God as you love yourself," and they unjustifiably do.

Buddha states, *"Don't allow the opinion of others to define you, for they can only measure you from their level."*

Need I say more?

The magical beauty that exudes from the colourful races is truly my envy. I unfortunately am like the dead men waking and I'm so white, I shine in the dark.

To wear my garment of freedom I have to acknowledge that my friend in the coffee shop was informing me of who I was in my past. I too wore those prejudiced garments of Adam and Eve, proudly.

To wear the garment of my new Eve, I now have realised that all the past life bigotry and prejudices of my inner white narcissistic Adam and Eve played an important part in me finding my new inner Eve. I have to balance me with this new loving and self-empowering attitude with my new breed of Adam and Eve's oneness.

By not understanding Adam and Eve's discriminations I would never come to realise Eve's graces. By understanding all Adam and Eve's peccadillo's, from my new attitude of Eve grace I am able to prevent myself from falling victim to their egocentricity again.

I now live my loveliness. My new outlook has to be my creative source. By changing my attitude to me first; my outside world will automatically alter and mirror those changes. By knowing I already have it all, I allow loveliness to flow through me.

I have a tear in my lung and it has prematurely aged me. However, I have been blessed with one of the best and brilliant medical teams in Australia for Thoracic medicine. One of my timelines was a skin disorder. I was dehydrating severely. I thought it was psoriasis. One doctor recommended instead of drying myself with a towel, cream myself after a shower, very productive and it restored my skin back to a healthy norm rapidly.

A simple cure without prescriptions, and it works, but I have to do it. The point is my ill health is a timeline occurrence I am re-living. My past and present are one so at the same time, at the same age, I procured a similar disease.

However, when I needed to create an alternative to my similar situation, I created this saving grace; the cream scenario. It was the assistance I procured for me to experience then and I am re-living that experience in my now. This is the results of how we read our past life outcomes in our now. You re-live them over and over again, in a loop until the lesson is learnt. Now I know and understand the true mirror of these theories.

I lost sizes, and went from size twenty to size thirteen only now to be informed, the medication I'm taking will force me to put all that weight back on again. I'm also informed I will have an edgy sense of humour. I may lose some of my mental facilities. My concentration may diminish, and an endless list goes on.

Through medication my mother lost her mental facilities, her bodily functions, her home, her finances' and finally her life. She was re-living one of my past lives. She was also my future feedback should I choose. In understanding the reincarnational timeline; instead of reacting to these circumstances, I know the outcomes, I now know I have better choices.

I allow the universe to provide all the facts to me either through friends or acquaintance. I then allow all the cells within my genes to all agree and gain the ultimate happiness and health for me. It will provide the path to everything I need to achieve my ultimate well-being.

I practice that; that is how the weight fell of me in the first place. My body of history, all of the victimisation both within me and outside of me, literally melted way and vanished.

My friends changed; my environment altered; my opinions altered; I became the new human image of these innovative ideas. I felt inspired about my new attitudes. They weren't prejudiced, bigoted, secular, racist; they donned equality, self-empowerment and self-love for everyone. I allowed myself to live it.

However, now there was this new unacceptable glitch. The possibility of me looking and acting like santa clause's mother or tweedy bird's grandmother was not on my agenda.

I have lived this before and am re-living it again. However, this time no one was in front of me explaining my direction. Was this because they no longer existed? Was this occurring to me due to a picture I created for me to experience, probably at this time of my life, in my previous lifetime.

-In other words, my judgemental supercilious interpretation of some old women in a past life (possibly deemed from a male's perspective) was this chubby, loud mouthed, obese female, whom I obviously detested and openly probably condemned. One image was the same vision as that of my grandmother. Her health near the end of her life was with excessive obesity and heart. She however was the pure embodiment of victimising Adam and Eve. -

Could this exercise be informing me that I may be on the same path as my grandmother and the ill health procured her. She passed away many years ago. Is her past path and mine now intertwined as an optional future; if so, then this is also my opportunity to rectify it.-

That's basic regeneration timeline creation, that's basic history repeating itself. However, in this life time I have been blessed with this information explaining that I am re-living a past life regression, in my now. All information is important. I now need to dig deeper to find an emotional injustice or desire behind my need for this chemical restoration and malformation, but I also know I already have the answer. I just have to wait for it.

This illness and the need for these chemicals to heal it, really doesn't exist. This experience is the result of some emotional injustice in my past existence, and it is now my consequential timeline. When doctors say a disease is generic, they are right but they do not determine why.

This diagnosis of fat genes is an emotional injustice I now physically embody. Those opinions and emotions, I am now wearing them as my garment in every single cell inside my body until I can find its core and alter it.

As my daughter explained I have a choice to be in victim mode or not. I can fight it or I can allow.

I'm constantly being forced to fight. I am regularly being pressured into being victim to a component of this disease. If I choose not to fight and allow, I lose the simple things in life that I have just again acquired; like breathing, walking, dancing, singing, laughing.

The obesity phenomenon attached to the medication makes the simple things in life complicated, forcing exertion. Too difficult an exertion may exacerbate the tear in my lung even more and so all my exercise has to become consistently monitored.

This part of my journey started exposing another inevitable path ahead of me. A timeline that was bigger and stronger. The timeline that was re-programming my life again to a form of struggle and victimisation.

My Adam and Eve has evoked the physical fight to survive instinct within me against all my better intuitions. Somewhere within me there was an emotional injustice fighting to survive. I was being vicitmised and sometimes you have to ride the wave to see where it leads.

This is a strong timeline. I have lived this experience before, and I am re- living it again. Did I react last time and accost an innocent old obese woman. Now this biased prejudice is the result. This time I am now allowing it, as opposed to reacting to it.

I was yet to uncover my real debarkle. Was it Centuries and centuries of indignation **against** me as a female or others; or centuries and centuries of indignation purported **by** me to females and others?

From an early age, I displayed offence, as I studied that some man-made God found me or anyone an abomination or a lessor being due to colour, gender, size because I lacked white man's education or ethnical views.

That opinion played huge havoc with my resentment against supposed scholarly men and the churches in my study of the history of narcissism.

It intensified my desire to stand up for WOMEN's rights. I say women for I'm talking about the voluptuous magnificently shaped women who are either coloured or white; who are sparking, vibrant and alive, but who are treated as lessor beings because of what they look like according to Adam's' and Eve's social media groups.

The women who have breasts, thighs, tummy's that lovers can get lost in. Bodies that cushion like soft pillows your lover's body all night long and he or she lays with you and does not want to let you go.

A body that is so scented with the most luscious of perfumes in every orifice, so that with every movement it wafts sexual appeal and enthusiasm for both parties to relish.

As women, we are marvellous looking beings even though our bodies of history are carrying centuries of abusive torment. For lifetimes we have had to tolerate the worst type of maltreatment and for the first time, in this life, we are physically exposing the type of ill-treatment we had to endure.

Through our feelings of emotional injustice, we physically cover up the damaged parts of our body that were exposed to the past life agonies and abuse. Big breasts cover our heart and lungs, sexual organs are covered by thighs and tummies; they are all covered due to past life shames.

Physical timeline feedbacks inform you of how much you hated yourself because these organs are the cause of constant intensified grief over the centuries due to the lies imposed by our celibate supremist Adam.

In the Middle East there was and still are laws and legislation where the women cannot be seen. I remember asking over twenty years ago why this intolerance occurs.

Later studies revealed that the answer may date back to beliefs from religious dogma regarding the abomination of womanhood.

A story told to me by a Kurdish woman was "the husbands see us as so beautiful we are not allowed to show our face so as not to stimulate any man, so spiritually by law, we have to cover up."

Common sense will tell you this is not a God given principle. Women are beautiful, soft and luscious, but the man's attitude is the man's problem not the woman's. If he cannot respect the woman then he does not respect himself.

If a real God was to portray beauty in a world and the universe, it would be this way;

"through the blossoms of womanhood."

But centuries of male prejudice still continued. If girls/ women had studied in Egyptian temples to be high priestesses of the goddesses; according to the narcissistic man-made ideologies of other mid-eastern and Asian tribal men they had the right to arrest, sexually assault, abuse, and rape them for they were not of their deity, therefore godless and soulless. This gave them the right to stone them to death. The duplicity was unbalanced and based solely on male egotism and cowardly dominance. Simply through their appearance, these women questioned their authority.

This malevolence displayed no authenticity. Many a sixteen-year-old or twelve-year young girl/child, not boy, could be stoned to death because some paedophilic old man was having fantasies about her. She, this twelve-year-old female **child**, *"bewitched"* him.

This allegory was enforced in middle Europe and Britain up to and including the late17th century. Their mythos taught that this innocent child was conceived of some evil spirit and was filled with demons.

The paedophile, of course, was innocent. It was the child's/woman's fault.

Dirty old men, young married men, soldiers, were and are still incapable of controlling their sexual urges regardless of age, and these barbarians donned the rules because they taught that the sanctified men were created in their God's puritanic image.

These dirty old men according to their spiritual doctrine were then allowed to rape the virginal child to purge her demon from him then she was either stoned or burned to death.

Still in today's age, 2000 years later, these principles are more prolific than ever. Many young teenage girls worldwide, do not want to have sex with their teenage partners at an early age and the reports designate many are forced, manipulated or even raped against their wishes to fulfill the teenage male's hormonal desires for supremacy through sex.

This is not a female problem, never was; this is a ***male problem*** and many boys and men need to learn some facts about self-control. Under some false presario, both still believe sex makes them the man. It doesn't. It just makes them huge asses.

I reiterate here, this is not a God thing. Do you believe for one minute this would have occurred, if women were educated equally 20000 centuries ago?

This lack of accountability has always given our narcissistic Adam a false sense of superiority and dominance. Through their misogynistic paedophilic characteristic, they then expunged themselves of any responsibility and instructed others of this disillusioned deception; falsely labelling the innocent gentler sex as the cause of their problem.

How could anything created from their God be so impudent? How could anything so brazen be of their God and force men to want to do the evil things they wanted to do to themselves as well as the women and children?

This impertinent child, woman is of Satan. This being is of the devil. James the sixth the master inspirator of the St James bible, was gay and he strongly enforced these beliefs. He encouraged anti witchcraft laws, supposed pagan killings by burnings and drownings. His personal sexual affiliations were condemned by his church and law. Lennox was his male lover and his love since his teens who left him his embalmed heart yet he is renowned for his bible.

If a narcissist cannot control you, they will control how others perceive you.

Women or coloured, were not allowed to be educated or enter any spiritual meetings where their future lives were being decided for them by these dirty minded, old, narcissistic, misogynistic, irresponsible wankers.

Anyone in their right mind can see the arrogance and ignorance created at these over testosteroned congregations. Young and old men alike were all carried away by some charismatic lying speaker who was very good at motivating a crowd into a frenzy and passing the buck. Now this leader was giving himself and his over motivated audience permission to behave badly, for it was the lessor uneducated infidels who were at fault.

Since the beginning of time our Narcissistic Adam and Eve has always found groups where they can manipulate and control. They love religious groups, charities, politics, schools, hospitals; They become indispensable. They entrap enablers and are set to manipulate the entire committee. They create their little bully club. It has been happening since before man created their first settlement in 12000 B.C.

Once they have their group of enablers on side and in agreement, the rest is easy. Now all they have to do was indoctrinate laws to ensnare the ongoing control of secular groups.

Many old European and English doctrines were enforced stating that women had no souls, were whores, sluts and prostitutes, married or single, for they bewitched men's minds. Within the marriage this bastardised law also gave the male power to "discipline his household," or abuse the females within an inch of their lives.

On some islands they would abuse their spouse, then drag them behind a wagon through the streets of the town to see her in her vicitmised state, because she spoke to a family member.

This law made every female open slather for all man's sexual fantasies for centuries, and it has always been deemed as Eve's fault; there's more.

Because the scribes, monks, elders were monastically educated and celibate they were also city dwellers. If a farmer informed them of what a bull did to impregnate a cow, you can understand how they would have seen this action as abhorrent, an abomination. The concept of this action taking place between man and woman was repulsive, disgusting, nauseating and that is possibly how the transcript of the virgin Mary becoming impregnated by an angel was written because Gabriel is a female. When Constantine's consorts advised him, it was based on these ignorant doctrinated teachings of yore.

Teachings imposed that women were solely responsible for all impregnations. If they fell pregnant outside of marriage they were stoned to death. This stupidity is still enforced in areas of the Middle East and parts of Africa today.

These women and children are supposedly possessed by demons. Many a Roman soldier would rape a young child and these innocent children would end up being stoned to death.

As soldiers and the dominating masculine gender, they gave themselves the right to genocide any nation especially the females from babyhood to grandmothers.

This theology engulfed the world, how? All the information is binary coded into every cell.

As the cells divided, regenerated and became whole again, they became the new generation so did the old ethos. They divided equally. This concept is evidence of the genetic oneness of all beings.

How a male either today or in the past, had the brainpower to believe that another human, especially a child around the age of twelve had the capacity to force an old man to masturbate and play with himself, when many children that age didn't even know what a penis was or looked like, is beyond me.

The horrors of that ugly appendage in front of them, followed by the horrendous pain pounded upon them when it was thrust into them, and the indignant male's mind-set believing a small child of this age and size would enjoy such agony, only expresses the sheer preposterousness of these rapist's ignorant mentality.

This component of our research divulged a definite pattern. In order for any acts of violence to be legalised, a narcissistic leader would always legitimise a criterion based on formulated lies against their enemy deeming themselves as innocent bystanders and victims, while the real victims were persecuted.

However, Karma does not judge the reason of why or wherefore the action is carried out, it simply responds to the actions. "Do unto others, for it will be done unto you equally to the same measuring stick."

Now they too are bearing the same physical historical timeline over and over again. Their bodies are enduring the paths of emotional injustice they too had to carry out due to these false ideologies created by some charismatic narcissistic controller.

Power, greed, avarice lust and money satiate these chancellors' desires. They set themselves apart like wagon wheels.

They are the centre cog and all people go through them. Meanwhile they play everyone against each other. The more contemptuous the narcissist, the bigger the wagon wheel.

They then charismatically explain to everyone how by appeasing their needs and donning them the power they need; everyone will live happily ever after. To achieve that, they have to capture all the lower genre, men, women and children and imprison them into some slave labour to build them an empire.

They pressure many prisoners to build sandstone temples, pyramids and churches, towns, and industries, in the name of some false God or King. Later it became war machines and roads for their country, but the bottom line is still the same. These huge materialistic monstrosities are to represent the peacock's powerful prowess and prosperousness to his outside world. The bigger the miscreation the higher the price of freedom.

Past history reveals the lower breeds of people, (anyone slightly different or non-caucasian,) have been subject to the worst of dehumanising existences. Losing homes, land, their own prosperity, their families, their lives for these false stone templed deities and their leaders.

This is where these puritanical misogynistic terrorists dealt their worst. Enslaving the innocent to both hard labour and sexual slavery for personal pleasure before they went to church on Sunday and praised their God of unequalled abuse.

According to their Gods, these coloured or tarnished heathens had no souls so it wasn't a sin to abuse or castigate them into total degradation for they were building a temple in its honour.

American, Australian, British European Mediterranean, African, Asian and Egyptian all corroded with this same hypocritical brush and not only feeling no remorse but still to this day find nothing wrong with their narcissistic supremist convictions.

These sandstone architects, church buildings, temple buildings, are the legacy left behind informing us of how the narcissist abused all of us to achieve their materialistic dreams of wealth and power.

Down through the ages, Adam and Eve's narcissistic instinctual personality flows naturally? He is supreme; he is like a God; he is leader; he is mightier; he fights for survival.

These dictators worldwide, would be the first to kill the witch-doctor for their heresy of their nature's god, yet, they see no comparison to their own paganistic prejudiced rituals and murders.

To render all my past life exploitation, I have to reconcile all my houses, all of them. I have to recognise that in every single lifetime, all of them are responsible for me being the person I am today. If any one of them failed to carry out everything it did, I would not be the person I am today. I have a choice. I can react to my past and continue on that path or acknowledge the perfection of it for if it wasn't as perfectly syncopated as it was, I would not be appreciating the realisation I'm experiencing. I need to embrace every part of it for to ignore any of it is to invite the return of similar victimisation.

The fat oppression of the obese female from my past and the individuality of the healthy woman of my present, I have to embrace both of them for without either of them I could not walk the path of this marvellous woman I feel I am today. I need both of them to produce me exactly the way I am. I have overcome thousands of years of enormous hardships and won. By experiencing the path of intense slavery, I understand genuine freedom.

I can now empower my new feelings of liberation and allow the universe to unlock the binds of all my past inhibition and let me soar.

I no longer declare myself to be a size according to society principles as that is defined from a divided synopsis of fat or healthy. To understand a svelte body, I have to understand the difficulties incurred with an undisciplined one. Now I allow both for I would not have this understanding without either of them.

I now comprehend many of my pastlife overbearing narcissistic components of Adam and Eve within me and realise I needed to experience all there is of my enemy for me to understand my ally.

I'm allowing all magnificent persecuted components of me to exist for without them I would not understand the imprisoning art of victimisation; I see how much I'm stronger, sounder, more resilient, powerful, passionate, fervent, brighter because of them.

I needed to walk all my narcissistic supremist Adam and Eve paths to become the most empowering new breed of Eve and Adam I can be today.

Adam and Eve still are individual embodiments of emotions that have evolved due to the emotional injustices of the ongoing world of the past. Through them I have experienced mass injustices.

> The embodiment of my new breed of Adam and Eve
> within me now and will empower my true justice.

I WAS DIVIDED

NOW CAN YOU SEE ME?

Chapter Six

I AM NATION

NOW SEE ME

Through the science of hypnotherapy, we, as in our research group, did experiments on the path of lies, then later the timelines and the damage incurred by them. One inference that dominated all others was, it is the narcissist personality's prime tool. This later invoked my path on the narcissistic value of pre-war lies and how the arts of war are all initially instigated through this labyrinth of deceit.

Constantine is renowned for the first act of Anti-Semitism. He joined together tribes of religious sects under the Edict of Milan, however the Jews and others refused to join. He proceeded to declare war upon them as a race. Many say there is no real historical proof that he destroyed many of their leaders and teachings yet the conspiracy theories have eked throughout history regardless.

Over centuries there were huge battles; many scriptures were lost and many lives were lost and many Essenes, Samarians and minor secular group went into hiding and vanished; These may possibly be the rediscovered scrolls found 2000 years later in 1946 as the dead sea scrolls.

One thousand years later historical data has recorded the facts of the crusades as a series of religious wars initiated, supported, and sometimes directed by the Latin Church in the medieval period. From 1096 and 1271 the Crusades refer mostly to the Eastern Mediterranean campaigns in that period who declared their purpose as *recovering* the Holy Land from Islamic rule.

The term crusades were also used in reference to religious conflicts among rival Roman Catholic groups, but they were mostly to gain political and territorial advantage.

The difference between these campaigns and other Christian wars was that the ecclesiastic inspired them as a penitential exercises for the forgiveness of sins which paved the way to automatic redemption and ascension into heaven as declared by the then Vatican.

In 1095, Pope Urban II an extremely ambitious man from wealth proclaimed the First Crusade at the Council of Clermont. He promoted military support from surrounding allies and armed a pilgrimage to Jerusalem.

The crusades were invoked for several reasons, but the initial crusade was the re-capturing of the holy city. For this impropriety thousands of Jews would pay the ultimate price for centuries.

Pope Urban of the Vatican City would retrieve what rightfully belong to their church in the name of their God; Jerusalem, the holy city. The martyrs who died or made it to Jerusalem would automatically be redeemed and go to heaven.

Across all western Europe volunteers took a public vow to join the crusade. Historians now conclude the combination of their motivations, which not only included the prospect of mass ascension into Heaven at Jerusalem, but also gratified economic and political advantage, along with feudal obligations and opportunities for Urban's personal political revenge.

The mass genocide and persecution against the Jewish men women, children and babies were carried out by soldiers, young and old who not only believed they were doing it for their God, but were actually capable of carrying out such repugnant acts for a God.

This overly ambitious Pope pursued a violent and costly campaign, leaving much desecration in its wake. Urban II would never know of his so-called triumph for he died ten days after the victory. However according to Vatican superiors, his policies greatly unified the Church, which may not exist today if it were not for his papacy.

Two centuries later on October 13th, 1307 Philip IV had every Templar arrested. The community of Poor Fellow-Soldiers of Christ and of the Temple of Solomon was founded after the First Crusade to protect Christian pilgrims to the Holy Land.

Templar Knights were arrested, physically tortured and abused and finally burned to the stake on Friday the 13th for heresy. All their wealth and property which they shared with their people, was confiscated by this puritanical Vatican basilica and given to their Pope.

These wars all had many things in common. Karmic continuum of same timelines, same impacts, opposite effects, enigmatic lies, genocide, ambitious narcissistic leaders, blind enablers, plus Middle to Northern Eastern Europe and Britain as the targets.

With Urban II, Phillip VI and Constantine the truthful influence of their invasions were never **truly** historically revealed. History always records them as the hero's when in truth, they lied and deceived for materialistic and political gain, greed, gluttony and power.

Centuries later during WWII, from 1939-1945 Hitler was an extremely powerful leader who could now commence his appalling retaliation ploy to invade and make Europe submit as he became the most powerful man in the world.

At the German trials after WW2 the truth about the Polish invasion and the Germans false declaration of war was revealed. Europe had said no to Hitler after WW1 in 1924; Hitler then lied to his lovely Germany as he started his full-frontal attack to make Germany the most powerful country in the world. He succeeded.

His narcissistic purpose was always his petty revengeful retaliation to crush these Europeans who defied him and rebuild his defeated Germany. He achieved his goal in record time. He rebuilt his starving Germany without Europe's assistance and successfully showed her off to the world at the 1936 Olympics.

In 1939 Hitler sacked his accountants who had improvised financial means to replenish his broken country by creating their own banks. They disagreed with his invasion tactics.

In August, 1939 the German SS police under the guided authority of Himmler invaded a German radio station under the guise of polish attackers. They murdered the German announcers while they were on air then manipulated and planted evidence to imply that it was a Polish attack. They also murdered a Polish antagonist prisoner then planted him as the ringleader.

Next day Hitler declared on air to his German nation, that this fascist act of violence was a declaration of war by the Poles and that justified his invasion into all surrounding enemy territories. He declared WAR on Europe

He declared his people to be the original pure Aaryan Nordic race; perfect specimens and as such rulers of the world and the lessor slavs and heathens were worthless human beings meant to serve them or be annihilated. On Sept 1, WWII started as Germany invaded Poland.

For the next five years they commandeered a savage retaliation. Everything valuable they could lay their hands on throughout any Jewish occupied townships was seized and melted down. Himmler's SS troops carried out acts of despoliation, depredation, theft, murder and destruction. They tortured, interrogated and intimidated all other living beings.

They stole centuries of art, culture and gold religious artifacts, belonging to all Jewish communities and cashed it in creating massive wealth for Goering and many greedy and gluttonous Germanic leaders.

All the Slavs wealth, their homes, their land, along with all the men, women and children were forced into enslaved imprisonment to rebuild his empire.

These innocent bystanders were unprepared and unjustifiably assaulted by a huge onslaught of highly trained soldiers, of Himmler's SS. History repeating itself.

The Slavs were imprisoned for many reasons. If they were Jewish, they were sent to camps to be exterminated. If they could work, they were put to work in underground tunnels to the manufacture more war machines. Others were placed in chemical warfare camps as "human Guinea pigs" for the testing of chemical gases.

Female children were animals, slavs and worthless so, were experimented upon like lab rats. After the war, large pits were discovered with endless skeletons of men, women, children and babies at all these campsites.

Upon victory by American, Russian and England, many of the survivors who were found had been starved beyond recognition. Their flailing skin was falling of their bones from horrendous chemical gas testing. Many didn't survive once they were rescued from the underground cells and saw daylight again.

Torture of the worse kind was donned on every captive man, women and child. Children were experimented upon by placing poisons in their food to analyse the effects the toxins had on their innocent bodies. The lucky ones died; but those that didn't have been left with constant debilitating cancerous effects for the rest of their lives.

From the beginning Hitler's narcissistic goal was revenge and power. He needed warriors. The adopted generation were created to build his army. Any child who took on the appearance of Nordic heraldry, who looked blonde haired and blue eyed were forcibly adopted and placed into the polish homes confiscated by the Germans and given to German families to be educated as the future perfect specimens for third reich.

Young women volunteered to become sexually matched with SS soldiers to breed the perfect specimens for the third reich and their leader. Once the baby was born, they were procured from their natural mother and placed in the appropriate homes for training, while the mothers were prepared to re-breed.

Once the war was over these adopted children and the new-born bastards were discarded like faecal rubbish. Many died from starvation and desolation.

Some were relocated to other nations, but all were deleted from the memories and abandoned from the Germans community's guilty archives.

The horrors of Germanic invasions, will remain with us for a long time, however, that was only one of the many atrocities against mankind last century.

That war involved Western Europe, Russia Italy France, England and Australia. Then America entered both Europe and the Pacific due to the invasion incited by Japan.

The true atrocity was the choices made by the Germanic people both during and after the war. Hitler narcissistically supplied his nation with employment, wealth, freedom and prosperity crushing inflation completely. He created wealth without money. The nation wallowed in their prosperity, gluttony and freedom. They refused to accept their responsibility and chose to turn a blind eye to the constant extermination of another populace.

They even agreed with it, utilising racism and bigotry as their weapon, later screaming innocence. The German crusade is over but the future ongoing loop of this war is inevitable and will still continue with the perpetrators and onlookers becoming the future victims.

The Korean, Vietnam and Cold war were other acts of mass destruction and terror and the reverberations of these slow mass genocide executed by leading nations is still echoing throughout the world today over 70 years later.

The controversy over the Marshall Islands is happening in our now. It is up to us how this outcome will transpire. For what we do now, will be done unto us.

Knowing what I now know and realising that this onslaught is visible in front of me I have to make a discerned decision. This timeline is a future inevitable path whether I like it or not. What I do now will determine what happens to me when I am experiencing that journey. It has nothing to do with the arena it is played in, it has to do with my reaction to it now.

This cold war, 1947- 1991 was basically a fight of the superpowers, Communism verses Capitalism. After WWII in 1945, Russia and America started the cold war

According to history, after America *successfully* attacked Japan with two atomic bombs, and flattened two major ports and decimated the cities and inhabitants into oblivion the United States government decided to test more radioactive weapons.

As with all wars through history from the beginning of time, the precedence is the same, to be the supreme power, the leader of the world. It starts with an abominable lie for the betterment of all when in truth it is simply a huge power play personally and nationally of gluttony, power and greed.

My point here is; if they knew their ruinous actions were going to reap the same rewards of opposite repercussions to the same intense value over and over again, would they have done it all in the same way, or would they have made better, more appropriate decisions?

As a reincarnation continuum fanatic, watching history repeating itself in front of my eyes has not only captured my attention but given me the opportunity to expose the repetition of the constant path of victimisation that keeps repeating itself.

What was done to the Marshall Islanders in the name of the cold war for world supremacy was unacceptable. The fact that the perpetrators now refuse to amend the infernal damage they did, is dangerous.

This chain of islands between Hawaii and the Philippines was a district of the Trust Territory of the Pacific Islands and was **entrusted** to the U.S. on behalf of the United Nations.

A high percentage of these detrimental tests occurred on the Marshall Islands, while other less damaging activity was carried out in Nevada.

The U.S. negligence is now endangering the entire northern region of the pacific, and all the information the world is receiving is belligerent excuses. If the offenders refuse to render their mistake, they will also pay a horrid reciprocal price, that's the way it works. History does repeat itself with exactly the same impact it is generated.

THE RUNIT DOME

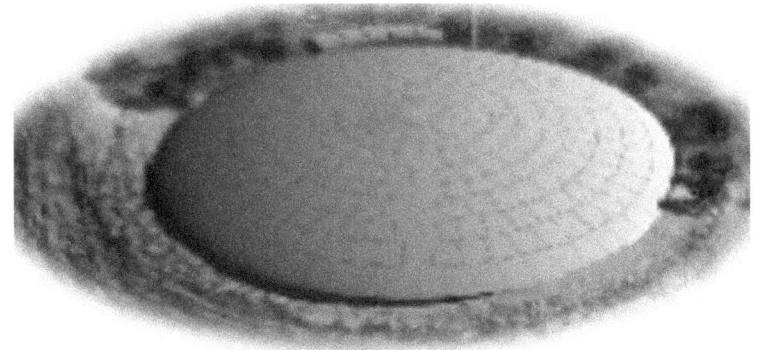

"THE TOMB" AS LOCALS CALL IT

Just kilometres off the west of the coast of America and eight hundred and five kilometres north of the equator, in the central Pacific Ocean is a massive, aging and weathered concrete dome plug which now bobs up and down with the tide.

"The Runit Dome" holds more than 3.1 million cubic feet — or 35 Olympic-sized swimming pools — of produced radioactive soil and nuclear debris, including lethal amounts of plutonium.

Two bombs, called Able and Baker, were tested on Bikini Atoll in 1946. Followed by a 12-year onslaught of nuclear testing on the Bikini and Enewetak atolls.

From **1946-51**, Nine of these bombs ranged from 23 to 225 kilotons, obliterating entire islands, carving massive craters into its shallow lagoons and exiling hundreds of island habitants from their homes

In **1952**, 25 bombs were detonated, including "**Castle Bravo**," in 1954 the largest artificial explosion ever recorded. It was more than 1,000 times more powerful than "Little Boy," which was the atomic bomb that *decimated* Hiroshima. Its radioactive fallout spread thousands of miles and contaminated both Rongelap and Utirik atolls

In addition to contaminating the Bikini and Enewetak atolls, nuclear fallout from the tests also rained down on and sickened people living on Rongelap and Utirik atolls existing on the outer part of the Marshall Islands.

In **1958**, U.S. authorities accelerated their testing. Due to the ban on above-ground nuclear experiments 33 bombs were detonated in a four-month period between April 28 and Aug.18 to beat the breach.

One test shot, Quince, misfired Aug. 6, 1958, and ***sprayed plutonium fuel across the entire Runit Island***. The *Department of Defence and the Lawrence Livermore National Laboratory*, rapidly ordered soldiers into the contaminated ground zero to prepare the site for the next bomb, 12 days later.

Soldiers swarmed in with bulldozers and earthmoving equipment, pushing the radioactive soil into the lagoon and the Pacific Ocean

Researchers recently found that the radiation levels on Bikini atoll were actually higher than originally reported, so more in-depth studies on the radioactivity on the islands were carried out.

They found external gamma radiation levels were significantly elevated on Bikini Atoll, on Enjebi Island, on Enewetak Atoll and on Naen Island on Rongelap Atoll, compared with the islands in the southern part of the Marshall Islands.

The levels of radiation on Bikini and Naen islands were so extensively high, they ***surpassed*** the maximum exposure limit that the United States and the Republic of the Marshall Islands agreed to in the 1990s.

Researchers also recently found that the islands of Runit and Enjebi on Enewetak Atoll, as well as on Bikini and Naen islands, had extremely higher concentrations of specific radioactive isotopes in the soil. The four islands had radioactive plutonium levels that were up to 1000 times more than those found in Fukushima and Chernobyl.

A Times report later stated that the U.S. authorities cleaned up the contaminated soil on Enewetak Atoll. This is where the United States not only detonated the bulk of its weapons tests, but where they also conducted dozens of biological weapon tests later.

Then the Americas underhanded swindle took place. **Un-beknownst to the Marshall islanders,** along with the atoll's most lethal debris and soil which was dumped into the "Runit Dome." they also secretly disposed of their 130 tons of soil from an ir-radiated Nevada testing site and unloaded it into the Runit Dome as well.

The worlds challenge now is, recent reports have determined that the concrete coffin, which locals call "the Tomb," is at risk of collapsing from rising seas and other effects of climate change. Tides are creeping up its sides, advancing higher every year.

Officials of the Marshall Islands have lobbied the U.S. government for help. However, the American government officials have declined, saying,

"The dome is on Marshallese land and therefore the responsibility of the Marshallese government."

Hilda Heine, the president of the Republic of the Marshall Islands, said in an interview in her presidential office in September 2019**.**

"How can it [the dome] be ours? We don't want it. We didn't build it. The garbage inside is not ours; it's theirs."

In 1972, after the U.S had nearly exhausted its military interest in the region, it invited the island leaders of Enewetak back to see the atoll for the first time since 1946.

According to reports at the time the Enewetak leaders "were deeply gratified to be able to visit their ancestral homeland, but they were mortified by what they saw."

These magnificent tropical islands that were images of Hawaiian Islands, were completely vaporised. Photos showed an apocalyptic scene of windswept, deforested islands, with only the occasional coconut tree jutting up from the ground. Elsewhere, crumbling concrete structures, warped tarmac roads and abandoned construction where military equipment dotted the barren extremely overly radioactive landscape.

The damage they saw on that visit was the result of nearly three decades of U.S. military testing and environmental obliviousness.

The length, depth and extent the U.S. annihilated this island, then they had the audacity to extend a welcoming hand home, was the epitome of unreserved narcissism and an insult to any civilised national leader.

The Marshallese stated the United States has not only failed to take ownership of the disastrous environmental catastrophe it left behind, but they also claim the U.S. authorities have repeatedly deceived them about the *magnitude and extent of the devastation* they left behind with false reports.

Recent research found that the American government withheld key pieces of information about the dome's contents and its weapons testing program before the two countries signed a contract in 1986 freeing government from further liability.

U.S. authorities didn't inform the people in Enewetak, where the waste site was located. They also neglected to inform the people of the island of the dozen experiments with an aerosolized bacterium designed to kill enemy troops in1968. Teams from the Department of Defence set up new experiments. This time, they were testing biological weapons — bombs and missiles filled with bacteria designed to fell enemy troops. U.S. government scientists stated this process would be essential, and later it was.

The U.S. came to Enewetak and sprayed clouds of biologically enhanced staphylococcal enterotoxin B.

This is an incapacitating biological agent known to cause toxic shock and food poisoning and considered *one of the most potent bacterial superantigens.*

The bacteria were sprayed over much of the atoll — with ground zero at Lojwa Island, where U.S. troops were stationed 10 years later for the clean-up of the atoll.

The Tribunal, established by the two countries in 1988, issued that the United States should pay $2.3 billion in claims. The United Stated Congress and U.S courts manipulated the circumstances and documents later disclosed the U.S. paid a mere $4 million for damages.

Had the U.S. paid the original damages; they could have had sufficient funds to rectify the problem. They could have sent in professionals to remedy the situation to prevent further ramifications, but they didn't.

They chose an inferior solution; did an un- professional job, and now refuse to render the mistake, which is creating global challenges.

In September 2019, the Marshallese parliament, the Nitijela, approved a national nuclear strategy, which called for a risk analysis and environmental survey of Runit Dome.

It was to provide an assessment of legal options for its clean-up and a new attempt to secure the original $2.3 billion ordered by the International Tribunal in 1988, which is economically equivalent to $50 billion today.

Locals remember that on March 1, 1954 waking up and seeing two suns rising over Rongelap. First there was the usual sun, topping the horizon in the east and bringing light and warmth to the tropical lagoon near their home, then there was another sun, rising from the western sky.

They say "It lit up the horizon, shining orange at first, then turning pink, then disappearing as if it had never been there at all."

Hours later, the fallout from "The Castle Bravo" rained down like snow on their island covering all their homes, contaminating their skin, air, water and food. Regardless of how much they screamed, there was no escape.

According to government documentation, the U.S. authorities came to evacuate the Rongelapese **two days later**. However, by that time, many of the islanders were already suffering from the acute radiation poisoning; their hair fell out in clumps; their skin was displaying third degree burns, and they were retching and vomiting profusely.

The logical reasoning behind this holocaust was because the Castle Bravo test and other tests in the Marshall Islands helped the U.S. establish its credibility of its nuclear arsenal as it raced against its Cold War adversary, the Soviet Union, to develop new atomic weapons.

Two years after "The Castle Bravo," U.S. authorities encouraged the Rongelap locals to return to their toxic homeland. What the islanders didn't know was the entire island was riddled with extremely high levels of radiation which Americans knew but, had alternate experimental and non-compassionate motives.

U.S. government documentation from that time reveal that official's argument was; *"They weighed the potential hazards of radiation exposure against the current low morale of the natives and the risk of an onset of indolence. We have never been able to carry out an experiment from this level before."*

Merrill Eisenbud, a female U.S official with the Atomic Energy Commission, said at a January 1956 meeting of the agency's Biology and Medicine Committee, in reference to returning the ill-treated residents back to their intensely radiated island;

"Data of this type has never been available. While it is true that these people do not live the way that westerners do; we are a civilized and educated people; it is nonetheless also true, that they are more like us, than mice."

The American government decided to go forward with the resettlement, so researchers could study the effects of lingering radiation on human beings.

This resettlement proved catastrophic for the people of Rongelap. Cancer cases, miscarriages and deformities multiplied. Unidentifiable beings were born neither male nor female, just unrecognisable things.

Ten years later, the real catastrophic damage started revealing itself in the next generation in 1967. 17 of the 19 children who were younger than 10 and on the island the day Bravo exploded had developed thyroid disorders and cancerous growths. One of these children died of leukemia; This was only the beginning; others were to follow later.

In 1985, the people of Rongelap pleaded with Greenpeace to evacuate them again, after the U.S. refused to relocate them or even acknowledge their exposure to any radiation. According to USA's news reports from that time, the Rongelapese were not at risk.

The dome is now leaking. American researchers, and journalists have documented extensive coral bleaching, fish kills and algae blooms due to leakages from the dome.

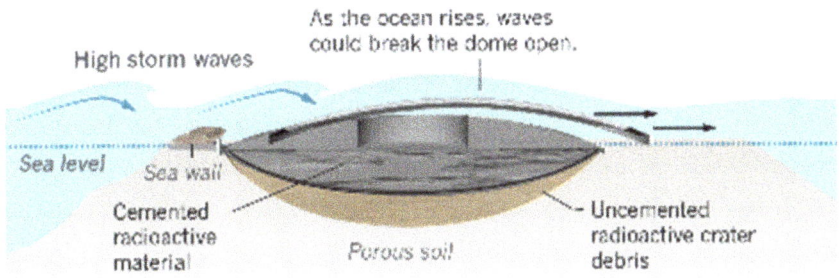

The Tomb, which was built atop an unlined crater created by a U.S. nuclear bombs, was designed to compress the most radioactive and toxic land-based waste of the U.S. testing programs in Enewetak Atoll.

This included irradiated military and construction equipment, contaminated soil, all refuse and plutonium-laced chunks of metal pulverized by the 43 bombs detonated in this 2.26-square-mile lagoon, according to U.S. government documents.

4,000 unaware U.S. servicemen were stationed to the area for three years to scoop up 33 Olympic-sized swimming pools' worth of irradiated soil and two Olympic swimming pools' worth of contaminated debris from islands across the atoll and dump it into this radioactive unlined soiled crater on Runit Island.

Much of it was mixed in a slurry of concrete and poured into the pit, which was eventually capped with a concrete dome.

Six military men died during the clean-up; hundreds of others have developed radiation-induced cancers and maladies for which the U.S. government again refuses to acknowledge any blame or responsibility.

The dome, constructed in the late '70s, is showing signs of decay. It crumbles; its radioactive contents are released into surrounding lagoons and Pacific Ocean.

The military stated they didn't know they had been working in a radioactive landscape. They mixed the soil into cement. There were no masks, or respirators, or bug suits. Their uniforms were a pair of combat boots, shorts and a hat. No shirts. No glasses. It was too hot and humid to wear anything else.

According the U.S military, "the completion of the dome fulfilled a moral obligation incurred by the United States."

Marshallese officials say they were never informed that U.S. authorities *had doubts* about the long-term integrity of the dome to safely stored waste.

According to a 1981 military document chronicling the construction of the dome, "U.S. government officials met Feb. 25, 1975, to discuss various clean-up options including ocean dumping and **transporting the waste back to the U.S. mainland.**

Many of the government officials present knew that that radioactive material was leaking out of the crater and they knew it would continue to do so," a documented reported later stated.

"But because this option was so inexpensive," they settled on the makeshift dome and relied on military personnel to do the cleaning instead of qualified contractors.

Later documents report that as construction teams were finishing the dome by capping it with an 18-inch concrete cover, new highly contaminated debris was washed up. They added the new nuclear waste to parts of the concrete top.

Soon after the dome was completed, the winter tides washed more than 120 cubic yards of radioactive debris onto Runit's shores, prompting U.S. authorities to build a small antechamber adjacent to the dome to hold the new "red-level" debris.

When it happened a second time, they built another smaller antechamber, then the U.S. knowing there would be more, abandoned the island completely.

Now the ultimate fear is occurring. The sub-standard alternative of the domes created by the U.S. to save all of us from nuclear waste leakage were never really safe and now these short cuts are endangering an entire Pacific Region.

The U.S. government's response of, 'It's no longer our problem. The dome pods are on the Atolls of the Marshall Islands, it's their problem now, we wash our hands of it."

This inevitable timeline has already been generated for them to follow.

It is our reaction to it now that will also deem our future.

*You will not understand what true leadership is,
until you experience what true leadership isn't.*

I WAS NATION

NOW CAN YOU SEE ME?

Chapter Seven

I AM KARMA

NOW SEE ME

As a child, two of the adages that were constantly shoved down my throat were,

> *"There will be poor always;"*
> *and "you are your brother's keeper."*

If there are poor in front of you, meaning poor in mind, poor in spirit, poor in body, you are re-living your regressional timeline in action. This path is not exposed to you because they need help, it is exposed to you because you need help. You are re-living this moment and now you are consciously aware of it. You have to ask yourself, what do you need to do for you, so this future path no longer exists?"

Teaching young children the old colloquiums of this callibre, and expecting them not take it at word value was the acts of manipulating guilt mongering nuns and priests who were emotionally blackmailing you to give them your tuck shop money for some clandestine charity they were running through their church. IT WORKED.

This adage although very true has a much deeper narrative and churches can't divulge it to you, for they do not know it. Their interpretation is, if you don't believe in their God you will go to hell therefore you are poor in spirit. They cannot extort money with the truth, especially from innocent children.

I don't want to be the one to keep putting the pin in your balloon but the facts are.

It is possible to make a huge difference to the lives of the victims of the Marshall Islands catastrophe.

It is possible to alter the path of the nuclear waste devastation and save the world from this future toxic poisonous disaster.

It is possible for a second time within a hundred years to elect to governments, young productive leaders who will forge countries ahead in paths of equality for all, without nuclear weapons, impoverishment, destruction and wars, encouraging equal opportunism for everyone; we simply have to learn how to do it?

By listening to our higher realisation at the point of impact. The realisation that all of this is exactly as it should be; everything is perfect. The realisation that at that precise moment we are re-living a past experience of opposite and equal impact. The realisation that we have experienced this karmic format thousands of times before and the ending is always the same. The realisation that you are the ongoing victim of your circumstances.

To understand justice; you have to experience injustice from every different emotional format. There are 7billion different emotional embodiments on the earth displayed in front of you today. You have experienced 7 billion different variations of injustice for thousands of years. The point of realisation is when you understand you are no longer the victim of those ongoing injustices. You now understand true justice. You understand that everything you have ever needed is already supplied and taken care of so, you will never need justice, for everything is exactly as it should be; perfect.

Justice, God, equality, love, peace; every one of these experiences have been portrayed before you to explain what they aren't; are you now ready to acknowledge what they are? You recognise you cannot have one without the other. To know justice, you have to also know injustice to the same value or it will again be unjust. Then you will be forced into victim mode again.

If you understand and you are empowered by both ordinances equally; then from this new point of realisation; from this new attitude of allowance, you can reclaim all your magnificent future lives and allow the universe to shower them all over you.

We cannot alter the old timeline of this already predestined fire, it has already been marked and is already blazing out of control, however, we can make a difference to the component of that disaster that concerns us.

When I studied the algorithmic patterns of the reincarnational continuum and researched how every individual emotion has a code; what we also discovered was a table introduced 10000 years ago that stated; within each emotional code was an average strain 444000 variables of that single emotion, morphed with millions of others at different ratios.

With further investigation into Buddhist teachings, we uncovered that they were speaking about how each person on earth replicates an embodiment of all those emotional variables at different ratios.

Transcribed that means you have 40% love plus 10% hate, 14% envy, 20% joy, 16% greed.

I have 30% love 20% joy, 15% anger, 20% jealousy, 15% greed.

I activate hatred within me so my anger is agitated but so is yours but only to your ratio. What you do with yours is your choice. What I do with mine is mine, but we are all built alike, just different variations.

So, that means by today's standards, there are 7 billion different embodiments of each emotional binary code in existence within you, all altering and evolving instantly, together.

In knowing this, you are now able to logically figure out what is actually occurring within your body. You are able now to visualise a mathematical matrix constantly altering and adapting to every new ongoing piece of information which is inputted every nano second; meaning you are seeing the universal matrix constantly altering, adjusting, upgrading and evolving.

This is the continuance in visual form.

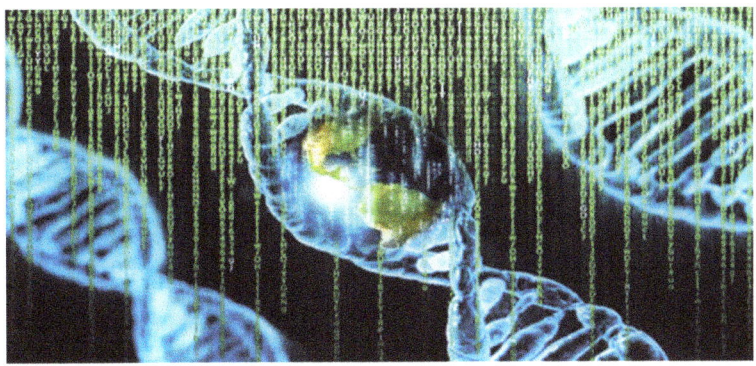

What has to be imagined also is, all that information is occurring within a miniscule cell of your body, that cell is sharing that information with zillions upon zillions of other cells at exactly the same time worldwide and universally.

Within each cell of the fifty billion is another fifty billion and that reservoir is endless. However, within every cell, every second of the day, a major alteration is taking place, due to your perceptional reactions, your judgments or discernments toward a specific situation or person.

Universally, every cell within you is equivalent to every cell in Andromeda and the Milky Way. There are more of them and they are sculptured differently but your reactional information is recorded within them at different ratios, for they are a part of you also.

Everything is automatically balanced. What we don't realise is, regardless of how we outwardly react to our exterior world there is an ongoing opposite and equal reaction taking place without your knowledge on the inside. It is your karma, and it occurs naturally.

When you are divided and you react to anything, you always react to it from the karmic balancing perspective.

If you are outwardly protesting against injustice, you are also inwardly declaring your next emotional path of that injustice. However, your original emotional protest 3 centuries ago may have had only 5 billion variations, in this life you have evolved and that emotional variable is 7 billion.

If you are standing up against discrimination and sexism you are also standing against the emotional injustice of emotional inferiority and physical abuse. This will be your next lesson on the path of injustice.

As you carry out your convictions, both sides of the information are recorded within your binary codes then your genetic codes then your chromosomes then your physical appearance. You physically appear as a representation of all your inner persuasions. Your outer physical appearance is what that emotional attitude now looks like.

Our old narcissistic supremist nation of Adam and Eve had one ongoing trait and talent. They believed they were the only ones that mattered. They believed solely in their egocentric individuality. They believed in their supremacy over others. They would take and destroy anything and everything in their path.

They too continually divided their emotional psyche, then expressed it and reacted to it in each life according to each emotional feeling; we all do. But this binary memory is cemented within us still to this day.

Today narcissists will always be conspiring with teams of enablers in the background somewhere finding ways and means to undermine all of the worldly peace and good for individual personal profit and individual capitalistic gain.

NARISSISTS ARE THE **POOR** ALWAYS.

DON'T SEE ANYONE ELSE.

DON'T HEAR ANYONE ELSE

DON'T CARE ABOUT ANYONE ELSE AND

THEY ALWAYS MANIPULATE THEIR ENABLERS.

The oxymoron of their attitude is; they need to enslave the entire world for them to *appear* to achieve their independence and equality. They are incapable of doing anything for themselves. They lack the talent, creativity, spontaneity and ingenuity. They are incompetent without their posse of enablers or their bullying pack.

Because they are emotionally divided, in their next life their timeline depicts they be the ones who lose everything and are destroyed. This timeline continues until it stops. The bigger the framework, the longer the continuation; person, town, nation, world.

Our challenge is our perception of time and space. We believe it to also be divided. We believe we stop and start. Because we don't physically see each individual life span unless we have past life regressions, we fail to consider that our lives are one non-stopping continuum.

Because we do not see the physical alterations that occur around us due to our bad behaviour, we disregard the possibility of placing ongoing safety guards into our long-term future equations. There are endless warning philosophies, but superiors have misinterpreted them to infer one lifetime only, instead of one life.

Eastern philosophy calls it yin/yang and karma. I only mention it this way because the knowledge of these two practices is already widely known.

What and how you saw, said, or reacted to it in the past; **is** *the opposite to what and how you will receive it in return in your time line in exactly the same way, place and time today.*

You **re-live** it today in the opposite and equal manner. You are actually living your past life regression through your looking glass. When in continuous victim mode you will do the same again at exactly the same time in you next life on the other side of your mirror.

What my latest research has discovered is just how exact and accurate those timelines are in reference to your time and space lines. Liken to Lincoln and Kennedy, the actions will be duplicated precisely but, the from different sides of the mirror.

When you open your mouth to protest against some injustice you speak the same words you spoke in the past. You are informing yourself of how you verbally voiced that injustice in your past life against you for you to protest against.

Now by emotionally reacting to your protest again, you will use the same words but your emotions will be upgraded, more evolved more expressive. You will then re-use this new emotion to upgrade your binary for you to move to your next experience to continue this new protestation from a different emotional context.

That's what is meant by "out of the mouths of the accuser comes the confession."

You are verbally accusing yourself of what you did in your past and what you will do in your future.

You may disapprove of a paedophile's behaviour. You express your opinion of the injustice against the innocent children, from your emotional superior civilised white narcissistic perception. At the same time, advertently or inadvertently, you are opinionizing how you want justice for the paedophile, he's inferior to you.

Your binary mathematically deduces your emotional opinions and puts them in play for you to experience. Your judgemental reactions in each life time will upgrade your binary to determine the type of emotional path you will follow. The justice you seek will be the justice you receive. You too will become a paedophile's victim.

As the timeline continuance of this debarkle unfolds from beginning to end it may take five lives. However, with every lifetime, you constantly re-live your past lifetimes; you upgrade and develop. You also have the opportunity to alter the outcome at any time.

As you react in each life time the emotional reaction is added, intensifying each step of your path, meaning, you can repeat the ongoing timeline up to four more times over and over again until your binary matches the path of the paedophile.

All paths are determined by specific binary codes. Murder, suicide, cot death, paedophile, cancer, child deaths; they all have their own individual emotional codes. When you follow a specific path, it has one determined destination. Should you question a specific path, your binaries will be updated in each life time so you can experience that entire answer.

According to further research from the past life regression from little Jon stated that you, "start again." When questioned further he stated 'there were options of the continuance or of finalising it and beginning again as a new soul.'

You can begin a new story; a new emotional path of injustice. You can keep creating them until you realise, you no longer have to. Then you can become a new soul.

However, every intricate emotional detail is mathematically evaluated to give you your final destination in the opposite way, at the same age, at the same time with the same impact. Although you will follow the emotional path of a paedophile, due to your emotional variables it won't be exactly the same. You may be a girl instead of a boy, you may live in China instead of England.

Like the gaseous path, it exists whether there is a fire or not, that is the inevitable path. However, once you make that discerned judgement; light that fire; you experience that path to the end. Your participation on that journey did not exist for you until you felt the need to react and judge.

The path doesn't judge nor evaluate your feelings of emotional injustice, it simply inputs all the information into every cell and provides your direction. Your feelings about the situation is what directs your ongoing karmic plots. Now every cell in your body will transform you into the human equivalent of your accused of your story. Over several lifetimes you follow every curve of your future timeline to the same final indiscretion.

You, within a minuscule second have declared something as lessor than you. You imagined the story in its entirety. Through your feelings you became passionate against this imagery. You imagined what actions he or she performed, and you made an unknowing judgement against all those actions instantly without even knowing it. It was so natural.

Every emotional inkling known and unknown is data and is entered into your binary DNA for you to experience as of the moment you made your initial conviction.

This confounding balancing act, although difficult to comprehend, is all instantaneous. It rapidly responds to the supercilious emotions executed by you. There truly is no true justice or injustice within the experience. It is simply your feelings about an incident that you have valued, graded, judged and deduced and matched with that specific emotional path. The reason this judgement has occurred is because of the binary of Adam and Eve within you; they declared themselves as the first human survivors. Its instinct.

If they knew that these actions of individuality would keep causing this ongoing separation from humanity would they have continued his path or would he have tried to find a better timeline for all of us. No; because they were fighting to survive. "Survival of the fittest."

When you comprehend that you are simply billions upon billions of computerized binary cells in human form; when you realise that your cells do not judge or criticise but simply become data; when you understand that you as that data are programmed to react over and over again to specific circumstances in specific ways, so you can reach a point of realisation.

When you as a consciousness are able to visually focus past the human binary formations; you are able to intellectually understand your higher forms of awareness; you are able to evolve to a better version of yourself.

The performance of a paedophile doesn't exist, it is simply another path of emotional injustice you have to experience. However, the truth is, it is all simply data, none of it truly exists, only the emotional experience which you choose to undergo, in the name of justice, and this is the only way this excruciating emotion can express itself to the fullest.

If you now understand, that by taking the path of the victim, you are empowering this individual emotion again by reacting to it;

If you understand, that this future timeline death was already completed by someone else; explained to you by someone else; and you can now see the final outcome performed by someone else;

Now you understand that you do not have to personally experience this path any longer.

You now understand that this occurrence is informing you, that you are actually re-living this past experience of immense injustice, imprisonment, and betrayal now. In recognising the intense emotional pain caused, you now appreciate the paths of injustice, and powerlessness, therefore, you understand the same path of freedom, justice and self-empowerment. Justice has been served. You're free. You no longer have to follow the destined path.

You are evolving into a higher level of self. This episode will now bypass you, and you won't participate in it at all. What needs to occur now is, in the same way you automatically reacted to all the injustices of your past, you need to automatically respond to the justice of your new now, by allowing all things to be, without thinking; without reacting, without asking.

You are not a paedophile as such, nor will you ever be a paedophile, that is the perception of the world's intake of this situation.

However, it is an emotional path of Adam and Eve's supercilious journey. You will experience the physical and emotional trauma attached to all their experiences along with others until you can appreciate what all these imposing boundaries are telling you.

You are billions of cells of information encapsulating thousands of emotional experiences from data dating back to Adam and Eve. They will then script, sculpt, shape and formulate you to be that evolved human embodiment of each experience of injustice. It is your syncopation of the binaries that keeps returning you to these situations.

Each existence brings you closer to your endgames, as buddha states, your real questions. Why and what you asked. And the final destination for you is always justice, equality, peace, love, prosperity and abundance, health, self-empowerment and self-love to name a few; how do I know this?

I now look around me and see the perfection of my universe being explained to me through the imperfections of the world displayed before me. I understand that it is being displayed to me because I created and existed in all of it. This was all my lives. Now I know what life isn't. I also know my inevitable future of endless happiness also exists. If I allow it to come to me and don't become impatient or anxious, it will all come to me, now.

If I question, I will push it away and experience every component of the emotional injustice I utilised to question with and that may take several lifetimes.

However, by allowing, you can now cease to exist in the world of victimisation and let that entire experience disappear by truly appreciating justice, or you can continue reacting in victim mode, judging and complaining about wars, impoverishment, paedophiles, abuse or murders in similar scenarios and continue on its inevitable loop over and over again.

The only person you are genuinely physically hurting is you. In other words, as your immortal author, you can alter the ending of your story at any time.

The people in front of you are hurting themselves not you by remaining in victim mode; same with the people following you, they are hurting them not you; so, you don't have to carry their burdens either. You do not need to take care of the poor; you are not your brother's keeper; it is their choice.

However, you; you are important. You are only damaging your prospects to a happy life, and you don't have to, not now.

You can realise that these wonderful people whom you are now re-experiencing your past life with, are telling what you have achieved. For at that precise moment, you are mirroring that exact experience live from your opposite and equal value with those people.

Your companions may be in victim mode and whinging, but that behaviour is essential, for without that miniscule deplorable conduct you would not be able to recognise the intricate binary emotions needed for this injustice to exist. Now you know not to whinge. Why? Because it helps create the imbalance. It's complaining; it's reacting; it's asking.

Now you do. Now you understand all of it. Your companion clarified it all to you. Now you know what justice isn't; so, you can truly appreciate what justice is. The more you look at your world and recognise how all the past injustices are being revealed to you; the more empowering your appreciation of justice becomes, the more you alter your physical appearance and wear your garment of true equality.

Keep your opinions to yourself, that is victim mode; that's asking why? Now you know; let it go. When you do, the emotional injustices of the paedophile experiences will no longer reveal itself to you. You're free to start again; your slate is clean; your world is rebalanced as one again.

That is why pain exists in the world. It was not created by some devil; You simply *felt* something was wrong and instinctively reacted and asked why? There are 7 billion displays of emotional injustice before you, and they are all informing you of all the variances of injustice displayed within you. In understanding all that injustice is; you should now also understand what justice isn't.

The precision timeline rebalancing act has and will keep occurring to Constantine, Hitler, Goering, Stalin, Urban, Idi Amin, Bin Laden and all the past presidents of America and the great scientific atomic research teams who betrothed the Marshall Islands to decades of unnecessary duress.

They will at the right time return to the world of their annihilation that they have created, several times. Their only challenge is they don't believe this crap.

They are educated civilised supreme scientists and superiors who declared innocent beings as lessor beings than themselves, "*but closer to them than mice.*"

Karma doesn't care that these brilliant minds who created atomic warfare for future generations, in actual fact have no idea what they have truly created.

All the presidents and all the president's men will now suffer at the hands of their own ingenuity by their predecessors with scientific brilliant educated minds. They will experience their own unbearable pain, agony and the lucky ones may even death.

They will lose their homes, their land, their families, their health and their lifestyle. They will encounter endless narcissistic barriers of deceitfulness and defiantness filled with obstacles hiding the truth. They will suffer decades of the same condemnation they exhausted on their victims in this life time. They too will experience life at the hands of some narcissistic instinctual supremist; the ones who,

DON'T SEE ANYONE ELSE.

DON'T HEAR ANYONE ELSE

DON'T CARE ABOUT ANYONE ELSE AND

AND ALWAYS MANIPULATE ENABLERS.

This is their measuring stick. They will receive exactly what they gave in exactly the same time frame as they gave it. They will suffer the same ongoing pain to the same extent as they gave it and when the time is right, they too will come to understand the true meaning of karma.

> *You have to experience all that powerlessness is; to understand all that self-empowerment isn't.*

It is through experiencing your ongoing mirror
That you understand Karma.

I WAS KARMA

NOW, CAN YOU SEE ME?

Chapter Eight

I Am Lying

NOW SEE ME

When using my original research, I was able to confirm that my life, in this existence, displayed to me the feedback necessary to explain the constant imbalances from my past existences that are responsible for my existence today at the exact same time that I created them. That was 18 years ago.

That past life research also revealed that, if something occurred when I was 40, we were able to define that this occurred in my past life when I was 40 also. We were also able to deduce that the same occurrence will ensue when I am 40 in my next life as well. This research uncovered the timeline theory.

It also unveiled the timeline pattern of yin and yang. The last existence is the yang of this yin at 40, the existence before that is the yin of that existence, then the yang, then the yin. All the yins mirror the yins, all the yangs mirror the yangs. You are caught up in an ongoing wave timeline loop based on the karmic laws of opposite and equal value.

By introducing my latest line of research to the already doctrinated research, it was exciting to uncover how another continuance took shape from all our past life formulas with new variables hidden with deeper agendas. I again asked the unusual questions of why.

Was I too, the continuous product of social victimisation? Reciting the words of the white man's discriminating tenets without question, then enforcing them upon others in each life, only to then be the victim of the very same tenets in the next life.

Upon consensus I determined that during this life, I verbally loathed the white man's supremist attitude from the age of seven. I probably disliked it before then but this was the first time, I openly stood up and spoke against it.

I questioned the dogma of the Catholic church and was chastised for it by a puritanical priest, who debasingly informed me, "ALL CHILDREN LIE!" Little did I know that I was re-living that demeaning occurrence with that priest, and his words were to be the very core of all my past life narcissistic attitudes.

In my late teens, I protested against the profiteering war in Vietnam; I fought against all Americanised and Australian racial discriminations; striving for equality of all sexes and genres. I protested against a cold war to no avail, not realising the full extent of the damage and human toll that was resulting there.

I walked for equality in Australia for the rights of the First Owner's to vote as Australians.

Later, we stood for the first owners to have their sacred land returned. This was the sixties and seventies; I was a mere hippie teenager.

I, like the rest of the youth worldwide was completely ignored. As a generation we burnt bras, wore flowers in our hair, sang protest songs, and opposed the wars, but the autocratic propaganda classed us as ignorant, drug taking hippies.

We were their young, protesting against their hatred which was deemed upon us and our world for the last century by angry old dictatorial men, who seemed determined to thrive on mercenary bullying of warfare.

All the world superiors were well over sixty; they hadn't retired as they were supposed to, and they permeated all nations with fear, anger, and guilt trips. They, Russia, America and Britain, just like Hitler, competed against each other for the superpower, to be the leaders of the world. They couldn't and didn't know how to work together.

They created international peace conferences because they couldn't communicate with each other as peaceful equals. None of them could be trusted, none of them trusted each other and they still don't. Their attitudes were all alike. They all assumed supremacy.

In the meantime, my private world was paralleling the same arrogance, but from a different fashion of emotional injustice. The older pugnacious puritans saw me as a simpleton, a rebel who was possessed and in cahoots with some devil or witchcraft. They also assumed that because I believed in love and peace instead of war and hatred, I was automatically fornicating anything that moved.

My constant walk of indignation was displayed through my being a slave to society's rules and family morals and ethics. These preposterous rules imprisoned me through my family, career, social activities, friendships, relationships, and marriage.

I was constantly having this inner battle. The battle of what I wanted to do verses the battle of what I was supposed to do according to society's rules.

Born in a time when the rules were "it was a waste of time educating women," for the minute you married you had to stay at home. Our heroes were the Nelsons, Father Know Best, all displaying the pretty little wife staying at home as the perfect mother. They didn't take our dreams away from us; we were never offered any. No one asked us, "what do you want to be when you grow up?" We didn't have the choice.

I never realise I was always living the emotional injustice of powerless, helping others, as opposed to helping myself, and allowing them take care of their own needs. I was always being preened as the good little sacrificial mother. I was always putting other's needs before mine. Yes, my generation displayed a definite pattern of victimisation, however, this was how the people around me relayed their love to me. They were my evidence.

History for me always portrayed mass abuse of females and children. The ongoing injustices of slavery to build protagonist temples. The eternal loss of freedom of innocent nations for power and greed of some protagonist, for thousands of centuries.

The mass abductions, rapes and murders of innocent children stolen from families to be placed in the worst of conditions at the hands of prolific slave traders for money. Innocents being forced to work for free under horrendous circumstances so some royal hierarchy could show-off their overawing superficial evaluation of themselves to an ostentatious world.

The enslaved girls as baby children, were forced into the fields, then exploited as sexual fantasies for their owners. As they grew, they cleaned their owner's houses, raised their children, cleaned up and fixed all the problems within the house for free sexual abuse.

If they refused or faltered, they were placed in a hot box for three days at a time without water or food as punishment; for these beautiful innocents were property not people and needed to be disciplined.

Once abducted, they never saw any form of their original family or loved ones ever again. Everything that defined them as either an Aboriginal, African or native being was stripped from them forever.

They became a new breed and now follow "the christian ways" of temples and churches praising a false God on a cloud outside of them.

This new breed has lost all touch with their traditional allegiances so much so that they also criticise the old ways of their heritage as heathenistic.

The beliefs that we are all connected as one, is missing in their lives. We are white; they are black. We are rich; they are poor. We are men, they are women. We are educated and privileged; they are powerless and forsaken. It is all fear orientated narcissistic power and supremacy over slavery; white man survival instinct.

Do it or die!

White supremist men believe themselves to be the invincible power. They are the superficially powerful, supreme beings and everyone else is lessor. Well, maybe this time.

My recent studies uncovered this stranger within. This phenomenon unmasked itself to me and it now plays an important part in our ability to overcome all failed actions, or questions as "why is this still happening, to me, the environment and the world?" The stranger is our Adam and Eve binary code, our ego code, within every human being. It's our original instinctual feeling, and it keeps defiantly manipulating our ego to survive.

This stranger is the original narcissistic supremist core code from our past within us that keeps forcing us to make our decisions from survival instinct. Your decision making is always deemed from the core of self-control. I'm better than, bigger than, stronger than, mightier than everyone and everything.

It's our constant ego based on the original competitive orientated binary of our original historical Adam and Eve.

I have a supposed theory; like the computer God is the original 0 and 112+ may be the original binary codes of Adam and Eve. All our binaries are matched with the original matrix of prehistoric man. The Neanderthal was our fighter, our survivor, but not our warrior. Our original binary is also attached to some barbarian; a titanic warrior, Adam. He gave no thought to any other thing in existence, but itself. He only knew one way and that was to fight, kill, abuse, destroy, attack and win, or die. It may have started out as survival tactics, but then as he evolved it became a stronger means of in-extinctual existence.

This underlying binary is the core code of our existences. All the histories and philosophies I've studied reveal this ongoing pattern of desperation, however, I didn't realise he was still my inner controlling ego. I was being manipulated by his underlying egocentric code of practice at every turn.

Re-examining my life's journey before I confronted my stranger revealed to me how this instinctual code constantly engineered its competitive underhanded malevolence throughout my life.

I always assumed I was making my decisions. What I didn't realise was the path was already created for me to make those decisions. My gaseous path was already paved for me to take this path long before I was born.

Driving home again, from the hospital, a song came on the radio by Billy Joel about the inner stranger. I'm quite sure when he wrote it, he didn't have my ingenuity in mind. I was actually re-living an epiphany moment. When the words echoed through my head it cascaded an entire avalanche of past life cacophonies in my imagination for days.

How can you live in one existence, and be another person in the same existence without being schizoid? How can you assume yourself to be one person, yet, actually perform and exist as another? This was my enigma; my new absurdity; my next unearthing.

According to my proven previous research, in this life, I had lowered myself constantly to the victimised mode of cleaning up after the debaucherous white species unacceptable behaviour; allowing them to take precedence over my self-worth, my health and my life.

This was my world of capitalistic imprisonment governed by men, for women in the world to exist in. Like men, I worked for money, instead of looking at it as a score card. I empowered the material concept and it became the deciding factor of my life.

This cold avaricious emphasis then determined my lifestyle, my career, and eventually my health. This was my predetermined ongoing timeline. This was what was re-initiated into me as a child in order to exist in this world.

This was also feedback of my timelines from thousands of centuries of this dogmatic ethos of the same principles with the same impact.

I recognised my infinity sign: I controlled nothing; My life style, determined my mentality, which determined my life style.

I worked mostly in the hospitality industry. Cafes, hotels, hospitals, aged care facilities and retail.

In the seventies this was a great career choice because it allowed me to travel and obtain work immediately, especially if I was a good worker and I made sure I was an excellent worker.

However, during that period this industry was quite possibly one of the most sexist industries in existence. The male customers automatically presumed female staff would patronise their sexual fantasies with extracurricular activities, and their wives automatically presumed we already had. I was used to this attitude. I was raised with this attitude.

The denigrating slurs and snide sarcasms from both genders of customers in reference to any sexual desires in those days was common place. Needless to say, many of the workers were not interested but that didn't stop the sexual harassment, which was legal then.

Even in high class cafes and restaurants, for a male to slide a hand up under the mini skirt of the waitress to touch the female's derriere while they were serving them was considered acceptable by the old drunken male connoisseurs, but not for many of the female staff. They saw it as most unpleasant.

I worked in that industry either in a bar, café or kitchen for nearly thirty years. It was my comfort zone. Within this industry I felt safe.

Although there were suggestive innuendos within the industry, outside the industry, for me, it appeared to be even more insalubrious.

I have always enjoyed anything to do with alternative thinking and different options. The reason I say this is because I would practice many of them as a form of escapism.

These amazing creative philosophies donned my life. What I really didn't realise was that these practises although spiritually rebellious and upright in their nature, were also part and parcel of my *fight* to empower that inner core stranger within me even further.

There is a quote I use and I will adapt it to explain this situation.

Your inner stranger doesn't care if you are fighting for justice or injustice; it only cares that you are empowering the fight.

My DNA binary must have been riddled with contempt for the white supremist species, their religious teachings, their infamous money Gods, for when I was born, I was the mental embodiment of this protestant attitude, only from the spectrum of victim mode.

The puritanic religious doctrines re-enforced upon me in my childhood was another past life regression I was experiencing, where I was informed of my past life allegiances as the puritanic narcissist and my present one as it's victim.

The time and place of my birth was also matched perfectly to achieve the greatest result. This information revealed the precision of the customisation of the matrix

During the second war in Australia, while our boys were overseas fighting for our country, the Americans were literally fornicating anything that wore a skirt.

Post war, this action instituted new rules by social networks, such as dances, churches, political groups, families and schools.

I was donned a baby boomer and I was one of the apprentices of this bombastic puritanical post war prejudice. No touching, no kissing, exploring of bodies of any sexual description of either gender.

Even stronger was the churches intake on the problem. **No sex at all**. It is the sins of the flesh. It is in cahoots with the devil. The only time you should have sex even within the marital boundaries, was if you wanted to have children, otherwise it was completely taboo.

These appalling declarations were force fed to me by my family and relatives, my church, my school and although I outwardly protested against them, for they only appeared to infringe the female's rights, this information was already imprinted into my binary DNA at birth.

I maintained this past timeline's dissertation. All these institutional boundaries were informing me of the bigoted personality I was already born as. This was my body of history; centuries of inequity and powerlessness hand crafted into every binary code and chromosome of this garment I was wearing.

Of course, as a child I didn't know that, and I continued reacting and objecting to the nonsense, thus, empowering, upgrading and evolving this emotional injustice and this tenet even more.

I was reliving all past occurrences however, in the past there may have only been 3 billion people in the world, so I could only react with 3 billion local new emotions to empower my then injustice. In this existence today I now have over 7 billion new internationally technically evolved emotional choices, because with each existence, everything evolves.

Everyone around me behaved with this bias, for the prejudices were only against the women. The men of my family didn't confine themselves to these imprisoning regimes at all. In fact, many of them had a really good time; just not with their wives. This improper behaviour by the men also added to my feelings of discriminatory judgements of their character due to their acts of unjustifiable sleaziness.

So not only was my environment preaching to me from birth about the puritanical wholesomeness of the female, it was relaying to me, that males didn't have to abide by the same rules, declaring the duality between the sexes of dominance verses subservience.

That's why bar work suited my lifestyle. It was re-enforcing the ethos of my past and of my childhood. It put me in a career of safety where dates were out of the question. If I went on a date, I drove myself to the date and took myself home, alone.

A huge awakening call to this dilemma was when my daughter informed me thirty years later that my ex, who also displayed and practiced extracurricular activities with gay tendencies within our marriage, stated to her that, *"Every time we made love, I fell pregnant."*

"How absurd; how preposterous!" I was furious at such an outlandish remark. However, after several more years of research and study, the possible penny dropped.

The algorithms and geometrics balanced, and all the possibilities and probabilities lined up. Could all the barbaric philosophies that I detested so much in my childhood be the defining factor of my life and my marital relationship as well. If so, how?

This possibility also revealed that my ex-husbands binaries would have had to syncopate with mine for us to function. That could explain why the only time he was interested in me was when I was ovulating. That could explain why his interests were outside our relationship as well. We were both re-living these predisposed elements of our past timelines.

As pointed out it is not our actions that determine our paths, it was our reactions to an emotional injustice that forged our ongoing timelines. With cold rationality, I was able to deduced how our marital relationship revealed itself. The timeline was explicit. It was inevitable. It was also quick, cold, productive; then finished.

We met in 81, first child in 82, second in 84, third in 86, fourth child in 88, separated in 90, divorced 92.

Yep, the ex was quite possibly correct; however, in retrospect of this calculation, it was more than likely the only time we copulated was when I was ovulating, or as we called it in the bar trade, "hot to trot;" indicating several things; like, animal instinct, fight to survive instinct and, or instinctively, I was probably the instigator empowering the subconscious false beliefs donned upon me as a child in this life and from my past.

Neither of us would have been aware of our timeline situation. We were both simply re-living and reacting to our emotional injustices through our paths of the karmic continuum of opposite and equal value.

This information was the holocaust that crashed all my belief systems of who I thought I was to the ground. It plummeted my self-confidence, and forced me to reassess the extent of self-control I thought I had over my life.

Those arduous teachings that I found absolutely abhorrent during my up-bringing and fought against so strongly, was the paving force that I was subconsciously living in this life, instinctually, without my knowing it.

This predestined path, like the gas for trees, was controlling my every direction. The more I displayed my indignation, the more I was empowering the very ethos of the injustice with a new emotion for me to experience.

Every thought, word and action I performed was from some emotional feeling of powerlessness. What's more; I actually *lived* that propagandised rubbish, and didn't know I was doing it.

Here's the irony of this entire situation. Every action from my family, churches, schools, career marriages were all informing me of what my past life timeline was and the direction I was taking, whether I liked it or not.

And me, the teacher, the trainer of all this technique of alternative philosophy, completely missed it. I missed seeing the real me. I saw the me I created; the me who was busy reacting and fighting and protesting and being distracted by questions.

"Out of the mouths of the accuser comes the confession."

My reaction to me then was, "you hypocrite." But I really wasn't. What I uncovered was every word I ever spoke or taught, was for me.

I then acknowledged, that with every fighting word, I was informing myself of who I was in all my past life existence and who I was going to be in my future existences, if I chose to continue on that path.

The more I fought against the discrimination of my outside world, the more my inside world was informing me of my true feelings within me.

It was informing me, that regardless of how I saw myself physically, I really was the puritanical narcissist. I was the one fighting against my past life only to empower it again so I could relive it in my next life.

The more I misconstrued the persecution around me, the more I was creating the very same angst within me for me to pursue in my future life only from my karmic mirrored perspective.

I kept over-reacting to each individual lesson with protests, till the real lesson was learnt. The timeline loops from my past continued over and over again until I learnt that I was re-living all my past lives in this life, at once, over and over again, with the same discriminating emotional injustices. I was on instant replay.

My family lied to me, and about them and me, from the beginning of our relationship as a child; then over and over again through our relationship as both violent and manipulating narcissists who physically and mentally abused me into submission. This was my first live past life regression as a child.

My ex lied to me about him and about me from the beginning of our relationship; then over and over again through our relationship as a violent and manipulative narcissist; his rage was exterior. He was renowned for hitting and breaking stuff violently. He manipulated me into submission. This was another live past life regression as a wife and mother.

Taking care of my parents with the ongoing narcissistic slaughter from her family, this was another live regression demonstrating all our karmic consequences of a family.

Narcissistic co-worker lied to me and about me to management about my work, (I was not the only one), yet, I still neglected to detect any pattern. This was a much later live past life regression in my career.

The acknowledgement that I was reliving all my past lives in my now and I had created all these experiences to expose my inner stranger who was secretly undermining everything around me, took a life time.

I saw my world as harming me, not informing me. I saw my world as doing it to me as oppose to for me. As a result, I missed many vital pieces of information, for a long time.

Until I practiced hypnotherapy on a regular basis, I had no idea that every existence I ever experienced was an ongoing formulation created from instinctual narcissistic lies.

Wars, philosophies, belief systems, creeds all of them from the beginning of my time as human have been based on all types of fallacies and false perceptions. Everything in this world is seen through karmic resolution; in opposite and equal value.

The world reveals all your injustices for you to see her real perfection.

All the new philosophies I learnt, were forcing me to fight even harder against these past life contradictions. However, my fighting was empowering the Adam and Eve's instinctual philosophy within me even more, sanctioning my future direction, making it stronger and more validated, moulding my future life as the egocentric puritanic lying narcissist again.

I thought I was altering the emotional feelings within me that were the cause of all my life's persecutions but there is one important actuality that had never shown its face before.

My Adam and Eve's egocentric ability to control my inner emotions, then empower one over the other, forcing me ask why, then re-living the answer over and over again, thus, re-living centuries of ongoing maladies of inequality and injustice.

This was the ongoing consciousness that was used to engage my fights; that ongoing struggle for survival that empowered my inner instincts to confront.

Through my opinion, in my past lives, I have instantly, without thinking, automatically assumed others to be lessor than me, lower than me, be it a murderer, a woman, a coloured person, a paedophile. At the same time my ego was testifying that I was more superior, educated and civilised.

The more I mentally and spiritually evolved and awakened, the stronger this incarcerating past life allegiance also strengthened the more this dominance to survive became my garment. The more confident I felt, the more superior I felt, but this inner essence of inequality and injustice was empowering me and I didn't know it was dictating all my future paths.

The more this instinctual ego was able to control my feelings, the more my outer world displayed to me the outcomes of those judgements.

At no time did I ever believe I would abide by the repulsions of those past life barbaric codes of practice, but the harder I fought, the more victimised I became.

What's more, unbeknownst to all my perpetrators, my ex, my family, relatives, church, and co-workers, they are caught up in this undercurrent as well. They too are re-living the same paths with me, over and over again.

The timeline indicates they followed these narcissistic devotions as well. Then as we all do; we exposed our past loyalties to each other by re-living the experiences of our past life over again.

Adam and Eve's instinctual habits were undermining all that I wanted to be. I had to learn how to alter my binaries so I could alter me.

I wanted a different story? I wanted to improve myself and unearth all these old constraining compulsions of Adam and Eve that had me bound?

I wanted to find a new breed of balanced Eve and Adam.

No one around me displayed any real form of love or respectful appreciation anywhere ever.

None of my generation were taught how to truly love ourselves for no one informed us of Adam and Eve and how they were constantly dictating this inevitable path of lovelessness.

You have to experience all that isn't love; to understand all that love is.

An iceberg was how I defined myself in this life. Although all the people around me displayed their structured family affections, none of them truly showed me love, or affection; including the ex.

It's not their fault, for when you see the iceberg, she's cold and aloof on the top, but the power of Adam and Eve underneath is bloody huge and freezing. The pittance exposed on top is minuscule to the huge driving force underneath developed from centuries of narcissistic egocentric dominating supremism. This was my real body of history.

My entire inner worlds of allegiances from my past lives had been reverberating from this conical of frozen stone, from bottom to top, from inner to outer.

I resonated like a sonar to the world and all these same cold puritanical performances returned to me. Every act of compassion and kindness I was performing was carried out from this ongoing instinctual attitude; from this strong resilient monstrous part of me whose purpose was to keep empowering this giant ice cube below.

This victimisation had been done in my past from yin perspective meaning I enforced the victimisation, now this timeline it was being performed from the yang perspective. It was preparing all participants around me to perform the same scenario at the same time with the same impact so I would react, to continue on my inevitable path, and I did.

A perfect example of this wide spread resounding echo was displayed when I returned home to assist my mother to take care of my father before he died.

However, she only needed me as the barrage to prevent her narcissistic daughter and sister from placing them both into an aged care facility that neither wanted.

Neither of the unrelenting females would listen to the aged couple, who had everything they needed to remain in their home till death. But the egotistic duo had more devious agendas to service their own personal power and greed.

Then after my dad passed away, my mother urged me to stay longer, for the very same reason again. She didn't want me there because she loved me, she wanted me there because she felt powerless. She couldn't stand up against her daughter, her son and her sister.

Their narcissistic onslaught was abominable. The light at the end of the tunnel for me was the oncoming train. We were both slaughtered.

We all re-lived this regressionary timeline for 18 years. This was our mirrored reflection of our past life. This period also displayed my soul-destroying powerless-ness. My victimised emotional injustice and emptiness. My inside world was being reflected by my mother's family in my outside world. I was re-living this life as victim to others.

This love was also the same abhorrent love displayed to women and other genres over the centuries by our supercilious arrogant Adam. This was the binary of my narcissistic Adam and Eve within me and displaying me as victim again. I was again automatically reacting instinctively by standing up and fighting.

After my eighteen-year onslaught from my mother's family, I walked away from all of them.

I continued my studies with my research group and we found many new answers.

I believed my new task was deciphering whether in my past I was the perpetrator or the victim. What I discovered was I was both. What I didn't realise was, who was pressing my buttons.

With each existence I evolved my yin/yang of Adam and Eve. With each existence I was empowering my Adam over my Eve from another emotional perspective of injustice, upgrading it, enlarging it, evolving it, until I arrived in this life time ready to empower him even more, from my emotional victim mode.

All my rebelling in the sixties was part and parcel of this path. I was empowering Adam and Eve for my future path as the powerful supremist narcissist again.

Yes, we stood up in the sixties, but the money gods knocked us all back down again and took away our hope, and our saviours forging us to fight more.

We achieved rights for women in the work force but not equal rights. We were later informed by our great leaders and presidents that, because we didn't fight in Vietnam, we as women, were unworthy of the same rights as men. But they were wrong; seriously wrong.

Eighteen-year-old boys should not have been in the Vietnam war either.

This action then again re-empowered Adam as superior leader of the world and all other beings as subservient.

Australia's hero for equal rights arrived for a very short period in 1972, when our newly elected prime minister opened universities in Australia to women. Hierarchy positions were open to women in politics, business, and enterprise.

Society introduced a new industry. The first entrepreneurial business woman. She was the backyard woman who, for a small fee babysat your children while you studied or worked. She set up her high fenced house safely with toys, swings and food. Child care centres didn't emerge for another twenty years. Eve was awakened.

It took over another four decades before a female was elected, but she was a woman in a man's world. She too was ousted by pompous ass liberal bureaucrats or money gods. But now women were being schooled, and in being educated, a new historical truth is being revealed.

In the sixties, American coloured races no longer had to sit at the back of the buses, but today they are still shot in the back unarmed in the middle of the night, by governmental authorities screaming innocence.

In the Northern Territory of Australia aboriginal children are being legally abduced in the back of animal vans and taken from their families. No seat belts, no seats, just like dogs. This government turned their backs. "Not our problem."

These beautiful innocent aboriginal children, are in our outback, are of a territory, not a state, where no one can see them or care for them. They too are invisible; if they put up a fight or protest, they are physically and silently brutalised to death; The police are allowed to further assault the adults or and abuse elders to arrest them under some white civilised law of that state.

Adam entices me to fight this situation through my supremist bureaucratic judgement. Eve utilising my emotions of fair play, they lure me to create a judgemental intent over that situation and then I will experience it all again through future lives of this supremist persona as both perpetrator and victim again. This is Adam and Eve's deceptional trap.

You think you are standing up for justice but you are nailing yourself to the cross. No, he is not a devil, he is your original instinctual binary; your dire need to survive.

One of my strongest wishes while taking care of my parents was, I would take care of them till they died and when they both passed away, I would finally start living my life my way. I had picked up and carried everyone for years, now it would be my time.

My hopes were, I'd return to social dancing and jitter bugging. I'd return to singing. Due to my services to my parents for such a long period the government offered some transition funds to help carers resettle. However, the greedy narcissistic money grapplers stepped up first and destroyed all my plans.

This timeline loop depicted that my mother and I be ousted due to a narcissistically manipulated family vote and this victimised stress caused by this unprecedented act of betrayal created horrific health disorders within me and as my father would say, "if you don't believe God has a sense of humour tell him your plans."

However, if this action hadn't taken place the way it did, I would not have re-commenced my hypnotherapy studies so intensely and diverted to this path I am now taking.

Do I thank them or begrudge them? No not necessarily, for this was my inevitable path. They were re-living their past also. It is also their future path. Their emotional injustice was directing them also. Adam and Eve were again dividing their inner houses also; we were all instinctively reacting to it with some new emotional injustice added, without knowing.

Finally, now when I have the opportunity to live my life the way I truly want, I have to fight again to exist. I am re-living a past timeline issue. I am re-living a past occurrence at exactly the same time, place, and impact as in my past life, so it an inevitable path, a predestined timeline.

My quandary was; knowing what I know; it is in the releasing of the fight that you gain personal empowerment, then, why was I always needing to fight?

You have to experience the unjust fights, to understand that justice is in the ability to allow.

All the injustices of the innocence over the centuries, from Egyptians to Americans due to this predisposed primitive instinctual disposition was as if no one else mattered at all. The opinions of the innocence didn't matter, their talents were abused, they were insulted, denigrated, humiliated physically, mentally and sexually.

Their rights were abused; they were more than ignored. They were starved, denounced, uneducated, thrown into pits, raped, and they were unseen as humans.

I have experienced billions of lifetimes but is this the first time I've been able to stand up without being knocked down or murdered?

Is this the first time I've been genuinely educated as a woman; not as a false priestess, not as a false goddess, not as a servant to the male gender; but educated in my own right as a woman, as Eve.

Is it like our education? It's not that we were powerless; it's that Adam never offered Eve self- empowerment before. It would have taken a very special person to do that. A new evolution of man. A man who understands equality; a man who knew his Adam and Eve equally within him as opposed to the Adam and Eve who are divided him.

If so then, I can also comprehend why I now detested churches belief systems so intensely and how I needed to find a God more appropriate to the needs of my new breed of Eve and Adam

Our new breed of Eve and Adam's God is bigger. It is in every cell of everybody equally. It contains all the binary information of all our past and futures. It is in every living and non-living organism that has existed and exists throughout the entire universes, equally for all, for all time. It does not judge, jury nor hang out to dry; it simply is oneness.

From this new amazing magnificence of my Eve and Adam, I am whole, complete and equal to all the oneness of all things even the white narcissistic Adam and Eve. I explode with talent, beauty, brains, all gifts from my God and I am not an abomination.

That could also explain why I'm caucasian in this existence. With my extreme repugnance for their abhorrent behaviour in the past, I would have expressed it and thus, altered my binary codes to produce the very abomination I found appalling.

This white skinned redhead in this existence represents a replica of some male or female woman whom I so strongly felt emotional injustice against in the past. An Irish woman who maybe kidnapped aboriginal children and forced her church going ideologies down my little throat.

Our body of history is not only the reactions to past life abuses it also exposes to us the perpetrators who deemed them upon us.

This is possibility why I had difficulty truly loving myself in a mirror? I am re-living my appearance of the human being who then in my past was informing me through their abuse of me, of further past life abusive timelines?

This image before me was exposing all my past life time injustices. My history, my philosophies, my allegiances; my principles, ethics and morals; my attitudes, good and bad and my underlying narcissistic Adam and Eve.

My Adam and Eve instinct of survival instigated this lifetime be in victim mode? I experience it more severely in each alternate lifecycle with a new evolved emotion. The intensity of that emotion played an important part in the ongoing continuum, empowering each reaction, then drawing me into various stories to experience them from that new emotional injustice.

When I read all the historical facts of the repression against women and other minors, I now comprehended how I could have existed and been exposed to much of the same brutality during of those times, because I re-lived it in this life; the Burnings, the Crusades, the Hundred Years war, Constantine, James the 6th, Egyptian slavery, American slavery and Aboriginal slavery.

I am able to visually translate how my binaries would have mathematically deduced the fighting emotions within me and match each equation with a future environmental setting with the same type of people, with the same type of pastlife allegiances and same challenges through each existence.

I then re-live every life cycle, through this intense emotional need to fight injustice again. I would have upgraded and returned creating even more deeming allegiances, enhancing, empowering and enlarging each barbaric situation against me every time.

As buddha says, *"the lesson will keep returning until it is learnt."*

That is why I returned in this life with all the same people around me. They are also being shown the same timeline experiences in succession for them to follow. Their binaries are the incompleted equations of mine. They displayed my past sequence of events and how I evolved. My binary is the completed equation of them. I demonstrate the journey they are on. I resonate through them, they mirror me.

They have physically shown me the type of person I was and the path I took to become the yin/victim in this lifetime.

In this lifetime I re-lived the path of injustice, inequality, worthlessness, powerlessness, abuse, victimisation, emptiness, aloneness, subjugation. These effects are of opposite and equal value of the path of Adam and Eve.

Although my outside world was exposing the results of all these past emotions, my inside world is fabricating the superior narcissistic egocentricity of both Adam and Eve and my fight to survive.

Now I know my strangers. Now I know their unrelenting fight for survival not only in the world but against each other and how they manipulated my binaries to continually fight against their emotional injustices.

In the world of Adam and Eve

you have to experience utter powerlessness and worthlessness to understand the beauty of self-empowerment and self-love.

I WAS LYING

NOW CAN YOU SEE ME?

Chapter Nine

I AM IMBALANCE

NOW SEE ME

Through all philosophies there is this constant Adam verses Eve, good versus evil, day versus night, light versus dark dating back as far as any secular religion will allow. It is eastern as well as western dogmata's.

This observation of the segregation of races and sexes is in all of them. These are man-made instincts ethos dating back to our singular cell survival. It is the psyche of how we evolved

The female body is sculptured this way because her binary codes depict that specific forms of emotional judgement together will configure this explicit creation. Due to ongoing instinctual binary information of victim, this body's program will update than act and appear as the new emotional injustices.

In all of the old Godly tenets, the female is always portrayed as the perpetrator of evil, wrath, anger and the darker side of the equilibrium, whereas man was portrayed as the bringer of life and light.

However, what is not written is, man wrote the books. Man scribed the laws. Man gave himself the right to rule the world. Men deemed themselves in a God's image as the most powerful rulers on the earth.

The other misdemeanour assumed was no other genders were capable of being educated. So, this fallacy gave supreme man sole reign. He deliberately only taught his male apprentices because God was male; In their minds they could not visualise how a God could spiritually empower any women's mind. So, they educated the ones who would follow suit; carry on their beliefs.

These hand written transcriptions date back to before bibles, and churches; to hieroglyphics on sandstone and images on cave walls. However, again, in all doctrine the female regardless of colour, race or creed has always been depicted as the purveyor and the reason there is all the evil in world. She apparently stimulated the sex gland in the male. She begets the sins of the flesh. Sins spawned from a devil and the list is endless.

Apparently, man was incapable of this. The parables state that if man, also referring to male child, is separated from females, he doesn't have these sexual impulses at all. He is the image of a God. He is the pure essence of the creation of the universe and the innocent victim He is not responsible for any of the vile lustful fornicational feelings, acts, the violence, or any of the evil perpetrated against mankind.

In their cocoon of silence and prayer where these pinnacles of parchment were being penned by these naïve tutors of truth; these scribes had no idea of the real world.

Popes, kings, leaders had many a lustful whore either male or female in their entourage but to marry them, treat them with respect, would deter their work from their God, who always forgave them of their sins. Complete chauvinist male hypocrisy, what's more many eastern cultures still teach these shallow tenets as fact.

Then these impostors of purity would manipulate nations of armies to murder innocence as they were not of their God, and thousands of volunteers would come from miles around because they believed that by invading another country and destroying every heathen in it would save their souls. Yet one of their mastery rules is "thou shalt not kill;" however, they were unable to see the hypocrisy:

No, it's not. Your kill any one, be prepared to re-live and suffer the same consequences in opposite and equal value, the same way, at the same age, over and over again until it is done. Is any murdering God worth that much hell? An ongoing repetition of the injustice as predator then victim, over and over again due to some narcissistic power playing instinct of survival for greed?

There are tomes and tomes of this maleficent prejudice, bigoted, biased, one sided nonsense, and after reading it, I had to ask the inevitable question. Why did women not stand up against these absurd and totally unrealistic accusations before today? Why did they agree, that according to male consensus they were unworthy, powerless and ignorant and only have one purpose; be a house wife and run a house and reproduce sons.

The philosophical answer is; Adam and Eve like us, are not humans per sae. They are the physical embodiment of billions of different emotional injustices being experienced through them. They are the physical manifestation of those attitudes exhibited in physical form. They both display emotional injustices in its physical form of predator verses victim. They are one. They both epitomise the injustice together as a karmic unit, and one cannot exist without the other. They through us and throughout this world simply display mammoth displays of yin/yang injustices.

To understand the true path of freedom, you must experience the tumultuous path of physical mental and spiritual incarceration and imprisonment.

Buddha says; "Don't ask!"

Unfortunately, again I asked; and I was answered. Then the psychology of the narcissistic syndrome unveiled itself to me and I began studying it in depth. I didn't recognise the connection for several months, but once I did, I then realised my little personal *fights for survival* were much more extensive than I originally anticipated.

My studies of the narcissistic syndrome also involved several murders that had to be analysed.

Some were so complex that the local police in European countries may have made some erroneous decisions and incarcerated some wrong people.

Others are so abominable and cold hearted, it was difficult to comprehend that in today's society, there are educated minds that have the insane perplexity to think with such evil dexterity.

This study became pivotal to me for it revealed what I needed to understand about my upbringing. I wanted to put my objectionable life into a box and be able to define it to a level of acceptability.

Yes, I have been seriously exposed to many forms of unacceptable narcissistic behaviour through my life, but, in comparison to many others, my exposure is still but a sprinkle of space dust.

Although through my counselling I was informed of my narcissistic debacle, what these studies did for me was to allow me to put mine into a box of a far lesser emotional degree.

This then allowed me to renew my research on a much larger scale of the reincarnational continuum utilising this new information and morphing it with history, philosophy, religious and political principles and deciphering a stronger more feasible theory as to why women did not stand up and defend themselves against the wicked tyranny of the narcissistic mind.

Women didn't realise that by not standing up and fighting they were using the empowering art of allowing; unfortunately, women weren't standing up because their preordained binary determined they be vicitmised and brainwashed from the time they were born to obey. The man-made laws stipulated they were nothing, owned nothing, (they had to give away our names) and were property. It was their father's duty to ensure they married well.

Women, coloured, subservients were not allowed to be educated or taught to read or write. So, to exist in each lifetime women did not know it was an ongoing continuum. To be accepted and loved in each lifetime women were taught to subject themselves to the binds of these civilised educated men's laws, regardless of whether they believed them or not. They never married for love, only status.

The men gave them a roof over their heads, so in return, the women had to take care of their house. They were taught to obey. If the husband died, they were homeless. Women owned nothing.

So, to say this leverage gave the male dominant patriarchs the free for all to create diabolical lies to cover their own asses isn't necessarily a sexist false hood.

If women were allowed to study and assist in creating those doctrines of those churches, politics and philosophies equally with men many years ago, the end results today may be completely different.

Simple things like understanding that men play an important part in the impregnation of women. Twins did not mean the female was in league with the devil. Twelve-year-old children are not responsible for dirty old men's fantasies. If women don't change their names when they marry, they too can carry on the family tradition.

Can you without bigotry or prejudice honestly state that the chauvinistic philosophies that are still endorsed today would wear the same prejudiced garments if women participated in the conceiving of the protocols back then.

Whether my statement sounds prejudiced or not is irrelevant, what is important is how these patriarchal philosophers were able to enforce their hateful egocentric judgement of bigotry upon others, then sanction it through both genders as law for centuries regardless of colour, race or creed for generations throughout the world was and is an act of horrendous abuse. As pointed out, it is not the outcome that has to be recognised, it is the emotional injustice behind it and the worlds reaction to it.

Everything throughout the universe is made up of zillions of cells in various formations. Even though you, as a human, are unseen and will never be seen from the Milky Way, your cells are equal to and as important to every part of it; as are the invisible cells of your liver an important component of you.

Every cell within you is composed of various emotions at different ratios; same with the people in the world around you. You all are sculptured the same way but with varied compositions. If I should activate a cell of hatred within me, the same cells within you and everywhere around the world plus the universe will react according to the individual ratios of hatred.

We, through an unconscious reaction to an injustice within our existence, create alterations or movement to the miniscule fractals in our binaries within our cells; creating further ongoing movement throughout every cell instantly; then they instantly resonate out throughout everything in existence.

What I didn't understand at first was why we reacted to the disturbance. What was the disturbance? The answer is this.

We don't create the disturbances. We react to it. Everything in this realm, reacts to it in one form or another.

The disturbance is our original instinctual fear. It dwells within your original binary. You exist because of it. The same as your cells for your liver exist within you; they exist because you exist; you cannot exist naturally without them existing.

But simply because your liver cells exist because you too exist does not mean you are liver only, but your liver cell will do what it needs to do to survive. You are so much more than just liver. You are so much more than the original cells of instinct.

The Adam and Eve binary has developed and evolved. As emotional binaries we are the evolutionary product of them, they are us, we are one. That original singular binary code is the corner stone in every person's genetics. It is our original ego. It has evolved as well to 7 billion of various nano emotions within all of us, and as the base cornerstone of our original binary, it will instinctively react and fight to survive in all of us, as it always has.

Now, because these ongoing judgemental instincts our ego created centuries ago keep reappearing in our timeline today, you are naturally enticed and lured into re-experiencing them over and over again. We then react to the emotional injustices again; assuming a new emotion; judge from that new emotional perspective, then we continue the timeline of the same with the new emotional instinct to survive. It then grows, upgrades, expands and evolves again.

I cannot speak for the consciousness of other cells, but humans perceive reactions and give them names.

Love, hate, anger, envy, spite, enjoyment, happiness, but what is mentally occurring is when like attracts like, we feel comfortable so assume the nice words. When the binaries do not match, we describe it with negative words, and react accordingly, but in truth the words do not exist. But your feelings, that emotional impact that you are either attracted to or repelled by, they are real.

What you are really doing is creating another new nano emotion. In the 1960's the four-minute mile could not be broken so they created the microscopic second. Now it is broken every milli second. 2000 years ago, it was stated that the seven deadly sins had 444000 strands to each emotion. Now like the nano second those emotions have been technologically expanded to billions of strands per emotion; 7 billion to be exact.

They too are ongoing and immortal. As our world evolves our binary emotions react to them, and they too expand and evolve.

As we feel, we react. We react due to our feeling of injustice. We activate similar emotions, like emotions but now we think from a different perspective than we did two thousand years ago. This new emotion becomes our new injustice. Now as old Adam and Eve when we question, we experience this new path. We have evolved.

When we experimented with life between life hypnosis, we discovered we were enveloped with this amazing feeling of unbelievable love and joy, or at least that is what we interpreted this feeling to be.

However, when we asked our Christian clients, what they were feeling, they responded; "Unconditional love. God. God is love. I am in God's presence. Huge human experiences of a Godhead and I'm in a heaven."

We then again, ask our atheist clients the same questions. Their responses were very different. They were more cosmic. There were feelings of unison, oneness, completeness, higher consciousness, harmony, balance; the equality of all things as one. They didn't mention love or unconditional love, or God, why? Both experiments had both genders, we made sure of that, eliminating the emotional aspect.

Then we uncovered the complexity of what occurs through our perception, through our emotional evaluations.

We, as emotional beings create according to our emotional consciousness and allegiances at that time of our existences. We physically embody those emotions in each existence. If you perceive your life through hatred, then you will physically, mentally and spiritually appear and react from that defined hateful embodiment of you.

Love too is simply another emotional reaction. We all individually create our attitude of a love to experience. Everyone's perception of love is completely different.

Love is like a fingerprint;
It is as individual as you are.

You cannot feel my love. I cannot feel yours. Everyone's interpretation of the feeling of love is as completely different to the next guy. It is your assessment of that feeling within you that makes it feel real for you and you alone to experience. You cannot give it to others, that is impossible. Your environment is also responsible for the way you interpret your feeling of love. Your interpretation of love during the twelfth century crusades would be completely different to the emotions you are feeling today in our computer age.

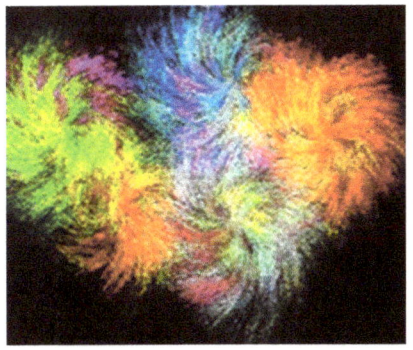   

MY PERCEPTION OF YOUR PERCEPTION OF
HATE, ANGER, RAGE. HATE, ANGER, RAGE.

From this new information it confirmed that no journey exists until we actualise the emotional feeling. Then the complexity of each individual's feelings of the same emotion, creates a completely different experience.

There are 7 billion different embodiments of love on the planet today. This then creates 7 billion different journeys from that same emotion of love, all replicating you, just in different ratios.

It is the dissimilarity of your perception of each emotion that creates your variance in appearances differing you from the Polynesians, the Africans, the Indians both Asian and American, the Aboriginals, the Europeans and the Mediterraneans.

The smallest difference of emotional opinion from yours by someone else, will reveal within both you, your new binary codes and genetic codes; creating a new generic chromosome for both of you start converting into that new emotional person within nano seconds.

This new development starts modifications in your physical appearance immediately, for the next life.

You may not notice the changes, but simple things will occur. You'll have to move, or the other person will move away. You will find a new job, or you will fall out as friends. Simple code alterations, upgrades, chromosome alterations, things taken for granted, invisible to the human eye, however they immediately alter the definition of your appearance.

You forget things or where you left things. You stop mid-sentence and forget what you were saying. You start going grey, your eyesight depletes, you put on weight or lose weight. You damage a toe or a knee or a hip or back.

All these upgrades which we take for granted are binary code alterations preparing you for the next step of your transformation due to some emotional judgement. When you realise you are altering every second with every thought and word that you speak, and you don't like the outcomes, you learn to allow and refrain from questioning

Your appearance refers to your environmental binary habitat, as well. This is what we call the law of attraction, but they are your outer cells your invisible cells adapting to the new you. You do not attract it to you, you generate it from you.

Every single binary within every cell including the ones you cannot see outside of you, that is your neighbours, all readjusted instantly as well. That is what binaries do.

They transform, upgrade, develop and every one of them evolves, even the ones you cannot see surrounding you. They adapt your environment to match with your inner binaries. That's why you move, you upgrade.

Using these philosophies our group was able to formulate research that unfolded why women had to fight to be seen for 20000 centuries.

A huge component of the answer was;
    A. the balancing act of karma; opposite and equal value
    B. the balancing act of the predator verses victim of our binary code of existence.

It is only now at the end of the twentieth century, from 1960 onwards, women in Australia and America were allowed to be truly educated. We were given the opportunity to become a new breed of Eve and Adam; He displayed before us the quality from a self-empowered human and the possibilities they could achieve.

But these empowering dreams were snatched from us and replaced by the same old superficial dogmatic archaism that froze our future potential in the first place. However now they let us, as women, stand out in front, creating the false façade of equality, when in truth, we are just men in women's clothing, still afraid to question their authority.

Then I take the journey back through my historical past, all of it is filled with this same diabolical contempt of bullying. America, Germany England Europe Asia, all my continents are inundated with this brutality, deception and revenge by my educated civilised lying Adam and Eve.

It didn't matter how much I obeyed my elders, listened to my churches or followed all the great philosophies, all of it was driven by and through this lying instinct of "survive or die."

The more I fought, the more I fought. I have evolved over 7 billion times. Each time creating a new emotional nano feeling, but still existing from the original personification of injustice to experience.

I have to accept and allow all that is around me for without any component of it I could never understand all that is within me.

Adam and Eve have to still exist as one. They are an important part of my learning curve. When I visualise them, I know what I'm not. I allow that.

I now understand that true justice, equality, empowerment and self-love far above and beyond anything I could have imagined.

You cannot feel it; I cannot give it to you,
But I have been given a special insight
That I can share with you.

I EMPOWER MY NEW BREED OF ADAM AND EVE
TOGETHER
NOW YOU DO THE SAME

You have to experience all that is duality to understand and allow all that is ONENESS

 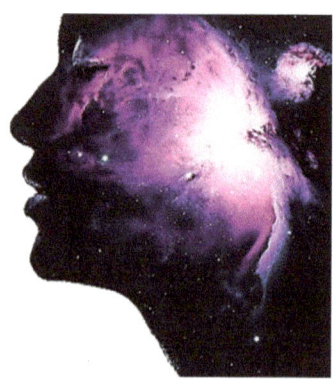

I WAS IMBALANCE

NOW I CAN SEE ME?

Chapter Ten

I Am Rebuilding

NOW SEE ME

Once you unveil this new empowered you, there's an overwhelming feeling to want to escape the old imprisoned you, to rebuild you from the start. Like my algorithmic friend who simply wanted someone to listen to him.

I regret that while our time together was short that I didn't allow him to speak more fluently without interruption. He would excite me so much I had question after question.

Now, in retrospect, I would allow him to talk and speak his mind completely, and simply enjoy his magnificence. My ego was competing for attention, just like he was.

I am learning to allow myself to be heard, by listening to all words that are spoken around me; I mean really listening; for others are mirroring me. Their anger, rage, unacceptable behaviour is informing me that I am re-living this moment now; that this is taking place again now, at this time and if I am not listening, I may miss an important piece of information.

That inner part of me that wants emotional justice. That inner part of me that is crying out to me for attention; the inner question.

The person in front of you in not invisible, neither is the person inside of you, so don't treat either of them with disrespect. We have to learn how to reunite both of them. The one in your outside world and the one opposite and equal in your inside world.

What's occurring now is, you are EMPOWERING **all** your inner binaries together, thus creating new information for your binaries. You are no longer fighting your outside world and giving it all your outer power only to be ignored and treated as a lesser being. You are quietly allowing and empowering all your DNA codes and chromosomes.

For centuries I have been abusing me, from both sides of the injustice timeline of Adam and Eve. For centuries I have been wearing their garment, their body of history along with all the physical replications of all my abusers.

Females were brainwashed or violently abused into submission. They were forced to adhere to the fallacies that they, you, are abhorrent, unworthy, soul-less, god-less, smelly filth, because, and this was the argument, according to the civilised educated man; women only had one purpose; bearing sons. They were incapable of physically fighting; incapable of harming others; incapable of killing others and were sexually in league with Satan. They were useless, worthless and unequal to men

As we switched sides of the bed in each reincarnation augmenting each existence to even more destructive behaviour, our conduct became more engrained. As we advanced our new emotional information kept becoming more embedded. We are all responsible for the advancement from clubs to radiation poisoning of mass populations of men, women and children on the Marshall Islands. We all carry this burden of destruction and the future destruction of our earth.

This is our egocentric warrior's evolutionary timeline, but where will it lead; in **our** total annihilation?

Only we can end this and it is not through further fighting or emotional injustice. It is through uniting my Eve with my Adam, your Eve with your Adam, our Eve with our Adam.

Adam and Eve are past life emotional binaries of our past emotional injustices. They are our narcissist verses victim. They are our superior verses inferior. When we embodied these emotions, we became one with them.

By melding the emotional component of me that is my Adam; he is my strength my power my male intelligence with my beautiful soft, gentle, funny, loving intelligent side of Eve, I become the best of both worlds.

My Eve and Adam are ONENESS of all men and women at their best. This means all their emotions are enveloped within me as one equally.

That's what we have to learn. We have to understand the one ness. We have to understand, there will always be pain; it's our reaction to it that hinders our growth or amplifies it. We have to allow it to exit but choose not to participate with it.

We have to acknowledged hatred for without it we would not understand love. We have to embrace every component of it for us to be able to recognise the smallest recrimination that may victimise us again in the smallest instance. We allow hatred to exist as it is, for without it we could never understand love, happiness and joy. By understanding hate we know happiness, love and joy, we equalise both emotions.

Allow your needs for material things and avarice to exist for without them you would not understand your feelings of lack. In experiencing lack you understand real abundance. You know you already have all you will ever need and are receiving and allowing abundance for everyone.

> Allow your weakness to understand your strengths
> Allow inequality to understand equality
> Allow victimisation to understand your self-empowerment

NOW ALLOW ALL THINGS TO COME TO YOU

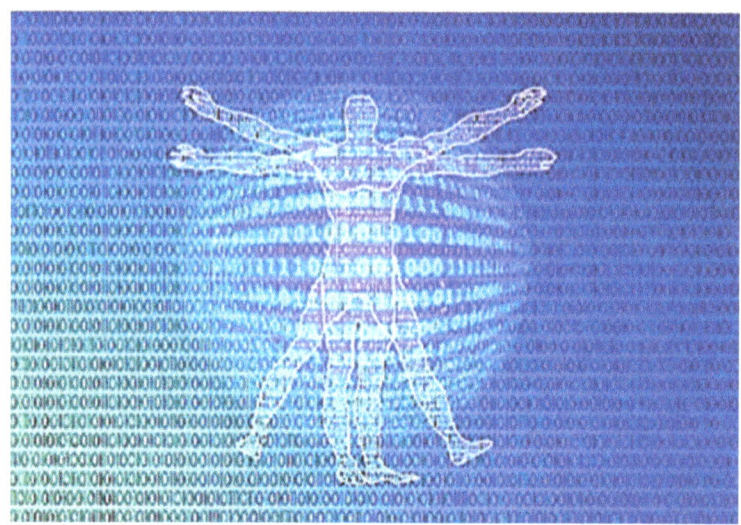

I AM REBUILT

NOW CAN YOU SEE ME?

Chapter Eleven

I WAS YOUR KEEPER

NOW SEE ME

Every woman should stand; and repeat this from the inner most part of their soul

My God created me as woman to represent the true epitome of ALL the beauty of the universes.

I AM ONENESS; I AM EMPOWERMENT; I AM EQUALITY;

I AM WOMAN;

When I was in the elevator and I saw that wonderful gentleman appear before me I knew we had experienced this before; I knew it was some sort of timeline prediction. I knew we were both re-living it again. Nothing is a mistake. Nothing is a coincidence. You never meet for the sake of meeting.

>Everything has a purpose; Everything is feedback
>of past injustice or future journeys.

"If you maintain your old attitudes this will be your future path."

I now have an even bigger responsibility to me than before. All the family members who crossed my path are following me. They were informing me of all the emotional timelines that bought me to this point.

Upon further examination, my challenge with this gentleman was, how far into my future was this episode of transformation going to take place. Due to his physical damage, it was very difficult to define his age or linear time, so I assumed he was around my age or older.

If he was older, then he was determining some component of a past injustice. If he is the same age as me, this information now determines that this action will be in my now. The tides of this timeline were expressing themselves within me as now.

I had to understand it or my future path would be expressed same way as his. My karmic path would be one of opposite and of equal value. I would be in his shoes and he would be in mine.

To clarify the timeline theory of now even further. A client who is younger than me by about 5 years decided to no longer be a victim to a personal friend who was constantly taking advantage of their friendship; she excitedly informed me of her actions.

Within three days I encountered the same incident with a person I knew who was doing exactly the same form of victimisation to me. We parted also but the happenstance was almost word for word. Upon her exist I recognised the egocentric narcissist within her and understood our connection.

We were re-living a component of our past when she was the perpetrator. Her circumstances had altered dramatically and now she was a horrendous victim of a narcissistic relative. I was following her, but I could not follow her on her path any longer. I explained, but to no avail, she wanted me to pick her up and carry her but I couldn't; she had to. I chose not to be victim nor be victimised.

These time frame experiments were uncovered almost six years prior when I was with my research group. The principles were still proving to be stable, however, now I am able to define the connection between the age and time link more accurately.

This wonderful client is a portion of my future path and I do watch her. We are both allowing an inevitable dream of the ultimate loving relationship. We are doing all the things necessary to accomplish this and one of the avenues to watch is our environment for feedback.

Recently a brand-new acquaintance has appeared with a new boyfriend into both our lives. He's lovely and adores her. She however, is ten years younger than both of us. My research for this exposé deems that this means the future possibilities of love is in the air now but not in the immediate future.

This acquaintance had to do several things before she achieved this wonderment in her life. She had to make huge alterations to her life. She had to move to a new address; alter her job; and obtain a new and different one, where she met him.

So, if the opportunity arises that I have to move, it would be to my best interest sincerely to consider it. What's even more productive is to start preparing for a move now. Many may say those actions are ludicrous, and that is fine by me, but if I allow fear to be my determining factor, fear is what I will acquire. I have to allow, knowing all is how it is supposed to be. I have to know this path has been created and I already have everything I could ever possibly dream of and more. This is nirvana's oneness.

If I'm to acquire a better future for both me and my future generations which are the family members who are following me, I have to work differently, think differently, unite my psyche and refrain from empowering material emptiness only and empower **all** of me.

If I am to listen to my inner self and treat it with respect and ensure its continued visibility I have to listen, honour and respect it. What if I do get it wrong, big deal, I listened and misinterpreted, but I still listened. I am no longer invisible to me, so either way I will obtain a more productive future, and the misinterpretation will expose itself again.

Understanding and constantly researching this information, I know how it works so, resolving my timeline from the gentleman in the elevator, I concluded it had to be about my actions now or very near future.

SOCIETY'S MARKETING PLAN OF DIVISION

My new revelation was, although I am no longer invisible to my inner world, and I'm outwardly feeling free, I'm still not overly impressed with the concept that the only way my outside world sees me is through their perception of my obesity due to these drugs.

> *You have to experience all that it isn't, to understand all that it is. But what was "IT"*

This was another inner emotional fight of injustice. Was I questioning my self-empowerment, self-love, self-respect, my self-worth?

In today's society to be recognised a woman, I have to bear huge amounts of indignation from marketeers who are simply promoting a product to create emotional division within women's psyche, materially empowering their low self-worth.

The ignorance of mankind does not understand that many a woman who has ventured through the outrageous abuse from centuries of violation are actually carrying their body of history, their ongoing past life abuse physically with them.

Many women will have been abused again in this life to re-live a past outrage to inform them of all the past life indignations both imposed upon them and by them at that time in their past.

They will undergo insufferable insults, sarcasm, discontent for this is what they did to others. They will endure the insult of scrap jobs as kitchen hands and cleaners, because they according to society cannot carry off the sex appeal needed to sell or deliver food in the restaurant.

They will be hired as the uneducated cleaner, the laundry person, the store person and they accept it because their self-esteem is so low that they also believe they are unworthy of any higher position or they need the money. (However, in these positions the money is good, hard and filthy.)

What is remarkable about these people is they are fabulous hard workers while the lazy idle persona of the narcissist supremists who won't get their hands dirty, take advantage of their amicable personalities and victimise them into doing double the work, double shifts, while they yak in a corner or take time off to socialise.

When the ship is sinking these hard workers are the ones who come to the fort to help save it. They will do extra shifts, work overtime at no cost; They are the reliable martyrs; this is the bartering of love they are used to. They are their own victims and consistently victimising themselves to be abused even more. They are everyone's puppets.

Their true self-esteem is so low that they automatically bend over backwards to assist. If they don't, no one will ever appreciate them, love them or even see them.

What's worse is, narcissistic management will take advantage of their kind nature and constantly impose emotional blackmail tactics to make them feel guilty, then as their enabler, the pressure is on them to save the day. This is their echo of their true inner perception of their personal love.

I am my brother's keeper; I am strong; I am capable; I will pick you up; I am a hard worker; I am a nice person; I am compassionate and caring; I will save you.

When they look in their mirror, they see a disapproving image. By world standards they are materialistically poor.

Because they are echoing some abnormal reference out to the world of unworthiness and it will keep returning to them references to prove it. They then will do whatever it takes to fight to prove the world reference is incorrect. However, it is not the world reference that is their true challenge.

They continuously walk in the world of "BUT" people. But people are Adam's and Eve's who out of survival instinct manipulate others to fit in their doctrinated boxes created by them, and you bend over backward to please them, "but" you never will; and they will always want more.

The enabler is kind, obedient, charitable, self vicitmised beings who will bend over backwards to don the "but" people's every need and be constantly abused for their efforts.

The enablers are always fighting against the abuse of others in any way shape or form; yet, they through their loving compassion and empathy, walk head first into the continuous cesspool of narcissistic victimisation on every level of their existence at its best and cannot see their own personal abuse.

They believe themselves to be helping those in need, not considering for one minute the unfathomable possibility that these darling people in need, are egocentric narcissists abusing them.

These marionettes will take every opportunity to emotionally blackmail and pull at their heart strings so that the enabler will, at the most inconvenient time, offer their total unconditional support, for if they don't, the marionette's life will fall apart. So, they keep taunting, guilt tripping and nagging until they get what they want at any cost; total submission.

The enabler will always find a way to resolve the situation at the cost of their own health, wealth, future careers, lifestyle, because this is what they do best and have been doing all their life.

This manipulative situation is then justifiably perceived within the enabler's physic as love and acceptance from a true friend.

Little do they know that the marionette's version of love is for the enabler to be their keeper; do it for them. They are playing you against others to be the barricade between them and their challenges, to pick up their pieces, clean up their messes, save their arses.

However, the second the enabler needs anyone to support them for any situation, Adam and Eve will play all others against them; they will abandon them, betray, ostracise and evict them. The enabler will then be thrown off the bridge and left to hang.

Then the egocentric narcissist has the audacity to return and without any remorse or guilt, re-manipulate the enabler into doing it all again. And on many occasions, the enabler does, because they believe this puppeteer is sorry.

How do you stop this viral merry go round?

The biggest challenge for victims of narcissistic abuse is to recognise that as a recipient you will automatically be in "victim mode;" apologising, explaining yourself, vindicating yourself always.

You are like honey to a fly.

This compassionate apologetic mode is the speciality of enablers. It is one of acquiescent subservience, bowing down, obeying, submitting and narcissists in all fields know how to detect it and hone in on it like fish to water.

Then they have the incredible knack of imposing apologetic situations upon the enabler confirming their lack of self-worth and confidence, while increasing their own confidence and ability to narcissistically control and take care of them. Romances are usually short for the narcissist cannot keep up this façade for long.

The first thing that has to be understood is,
the enabler has to recognise that;

ENABLERS LIVE IN VICTIM MODE;

You cannot and never will alter the narcissist perspective on life, they are in constant supremist survival mode but, you can alter your reaction to them. However, before you do, you have to know the real rules.

If you want to remain an enabler, then allow your compassion and empathy for your family, friends, co-workers and the world situation outside of you to be abusive to you. If you truly feel this is love and you cannot or do not want to be left alone, that is your choice and it is allowed.

However, if you don't, you have to listen to the real rules.

"YOU CANNOT HELP ANYONE ELSE; THEY HAVE TO.
YOU CAN ONLY HELP YOURSELF. YOU HAVE TO.
YOU ARE NOT YOUR BROTHER'S KEEPER; THEY ARE.

These rules apply to everyone around you, as well, especially your family, friends and co-workers, not just you.

Your point of realisation is; you have experienced all that wretchedness has to offer. You have experience love at its worst, most painful, most abusive, most arrogant, and thanks to that abhorrent person who did this to you, you are now able to appreciate the amazing beautiful and brilliant wondrousness of who you really are. Now you understand you already have all the love you ever deserved all you have to do is allow it to come to you.

You don't need them in your life but you do need to allow the memory of all the anxiety and pain they put you through, for it will be your tower of strength as you realise, you needed their bad behaviour to always understand your true magnificence.

Every component of that abuse had to be carried out precisely as it was for you to reach the level of understanding you have conquered. You understand you re-lived this exact path of your past life behaviours in opposite and equal value. It wasn't done to you; it was done for you.

Now you understand all lurks and perks of all this bad behaviour and when it appears to challenge you again you realise this is a past component you cannot alter but you certainly can alter your future outcomes by not reacting to it.

How do you stop it?

YOU SAY "NO."

The most magical word my daughter ever taught me to say.

"NO."

Love them; but love yourself more. You've lived
that path before; you know how it ends.

You understand all the paths now; the marionette and the puppet. They were both you; neither is more powerful than the other; you however, empowered them against each other within you and experience all that these powerless emotions had to offer until you understood. That may have taken up to seven lifetimes.

You've been fighting this since the beginning of your time. Your fight or your crusade for or against your right to be truly loved; your constant lack of self-worth, due to emotional injustices imposed by Adam and Eve.

Over the centuries the more you fought the more you actually energised it, upgraded it, developed it, evolving it to each new level of dissention for you to re-experience again from another perspective.

However, this time you met your waterloo. You are on the final receiving end of all your past life peccadilloes. They have done their course. What you were showing yourself was; in your past, you had no choice; you were powerless. You either stood back or stood up to fight again only to be abused, knocked down or extinguished.

Now for the first time in all your existences you are understanding the truth.

You created all this. You through all those divided powerless lies told to you by those elders who wrote those laws, those books, those creeds; created with your emotional imagination a timeline of what you believed you to be and with each existence you divided yourself more and more for over 20000 centuries.

To alter it you have to rewrite your new story for YOU to experience. You have to upgrade your feelings of emotional injustice to new ones of empowerment. You will want to alter your appearance, your attitude, your life style, and the way you truly want to be perceived by you to YOUR world. Why? After 200000 years you are no longer in the victim mode of Adam and Eve

MEET YOUR NEW EMPOWERED EVE AND ADAM.

The more you do this the more you see the ones who are representing your future path, excel with brilliance and amazing happiness. You then realise you have nothing to ever worry about again because your future path is more secure than you ever dreamed it could be. Now you can just be extremely happy and allow the happiness you *never* experienced to come to you.

People who put you in their boxes love you the way they want to love you according to their rules. This has been your past life for centuries. If you ever stood up against authority in any way or means, your husband would be told "Get your house in order." So, you would be silenced.

Our emancipation in the seventies allowed women to be educated and be able to utilise their education to reveal all the abuse that has been imposed upon us by our sadistic past life narcissists. We were given a new found freedom.

I was a teenager when I re-lived this. But it would take another forty years for me to be able to appreciate it.

As Buddhas says;

"Don't allow the opinions of others to define you."

What I didn't realise was, it was always my opinion of me that was defining me.

That quote should read

Don't allow your past life opinion of you to define your future lives.

When Gough Whitlam freed Australian women I had already been educated. The keys had been made, but the doors weren't open as quickly as one would have liked. I would not have called my life career orientated for I didn't acquire the degrees I needed for another thirty years

Now thirty-five years later, I am able to say to my grand-daughter, "what would you like to be when you grow up?

She can be anything she wants to be. She can go anywhere she wants to go. She can do whatever she wants to do there is nothing stopping her.

It took me two thirds of my life to SEE that there was a much better love out there for me to experience. It took me just as long to realise, I **deserved** a much better love than the love that was being displayed by the world I defined for me and all the people around me.

Family, friends, co-workers, all placed me in their narcissistic victimised boxes and they could only stand me in small doses because my innovative ideas did not concur with theirs.

Others claiming to be friends would visit me to receive the information they needed to help them acquire specific needs, material things, they wanted, then depart for months at a time. Then, they'd return for more, months later and depart again. I became their guru as well as their spiritual crutch. They needed me to make them feel better about themselves because they couldn't stand up on their own; neither could I.

Now years later with my new understanding of who I truly am I am re-defining me and my interests from an even more inspiring attitude. I am my new empowered Eve and Adam.

I am a free woman, a speaker and an author sharing this invigorating information for a specific niche of people who are matched with my outer binaries. In understanding that my books are already sold before I write them, I can allow all the inspiration to come to me the way it chooses. By allowing the research to come to me; by allowing the characters to come to me; by allowing the title to come to me; by allowing my creativity to flow through me; I am able to produce a book beyond my wildest realisation. I'm allowing my dream.

My invisible outer cells are matching and uniting everyone that wants to know this information to find it through me.

I now express ONENESS. I understand oneness, not in a godly spiritual manner like the nineties, but the real way; within me, within us, unison.

The study of the reincarnational continuum and its timelines absolutely absorbs me on every level of intelligence. It was and is the only thing that truly clarifies all my past existences, allegiances and karma and why I experienced my life as I did.

I see and analyse it in everything, always finding conclusive evidence of my challenges, then I have the opportunity to allow happier future existences and let them come to me.

Especially in today's age with computer technology and all the comeuppance that is taking place worldwide, I'm in the position to mathematically cross reference many past historical events with other situations that have taken place and deduce how history does constantly have timelines and repeats itself. Then I realise I have just re-lived another past life regression. It's exciting to hold time in your hands.

Now you know the only reason history keeps repeating itself is because we keep creating the historical timelines through our reactions. In creating our history, we keep reacting to each other by fighting and empowering the very allegiances that keeps us repeating the same things over and over again with opposite and equal effects.

By understanding our past life history, we can understand the emotional injustices that were binding us, burying us, hiding us. Every ounce of pain, anguish, isolation, loneliness, abandonment that you feel for the outside world is informing you that you are re-living an experience from your past, only in opposite and equal value. The more this knowledge comes naturally to you and you don't have to think about your responses, the faster you allow, the happier you become.

Buddha explained this information over 2000 years ago so this information isn't new, it simply now has been upgraded to a new computerised format, and women can not only learn it, but utilise and question it.

So, to alter me from my past life definition of me as powerless, worthless and a narcissist enabler; a new enthusiasm overwhelmed me. By acknowledging both sides of me I am taking me from victim mode and allowing freedom mode. I'm taking me to a more self-empowered, self-loved, entrepreneur and I liked it.

If you have to alter one perception to another it is like altering an addiction. You cannot stop addictions; you can, however, allow a stronger drive to come to you. Giving up cake for healthy food and gym. You have to find that something special to satisfy that insatiable urge from all sides; physical, mental and emotional.

So, for me to overcome many a sweet tooth addiction, I had to reach much deeper. I was informed I'm was an emotional eater. Lesson one, what emotion urges me to want to eat food? Answer, all of them. My list was endless.

Lesson number two; I had to overcome the opinion of my physical body; all size 22 of it.

I disliked my appearance harshly because by societies standards I was severely overweight and unacceptable. To be accepted by society I had to look like a twelve-year-old boy.

Even at the age of twelve I didn't look like that. At puberty, thyroid kicked in and I blossomed to size 16 in a very short period of time. In those days it was ignored by physicians as puberty blues.

From that day on I had to **mentally fight** for personal acceptance to prove myself worthy of my existence. *My opinion of me defined me.* There were no nice clothes for a child my size, then, hence, the loathing fighter stepped up and so did the victim.

Michelangelo stated that David was always in the huge block of marble; he just had to find it.

After nearly five decades of being everybody else's puppet, I finally informed myself, I cannot alter the past, but "this beautiful woman, this remarkable female physique was a precision piece of atomised sculpture" and just like Michelangelo, I now had to find my beautiful ME, inside me.

That was not going to be an easy quest. After sixty years of constant denigrating, disrespect both to me and around me; to alter the very cornerstone of my perception of me was going to take, that total overhaul.

I was lucky. I understood reincarnation and had visualised many different forms of feedback from my family alone, dating back three generations, plus verbal history even further.

I was able to graphically read my past life progress through their chronological existences, their reactions and their responses to each other and me.

I was able to read the violence, the narcissism, the greed, the politics, the puritanical religious infractions, the bigotry, sexism, racism, theft, war, jealousy and envy of my genetic heritage.

I was able to file their performances in chronological order to see their imbalances and future outcomes, then deduce my timelines.

Although their lives or the arenas they played in would have physically varied to the original, the driving force behind all of them was based on the same narcissistic allegiances, self-loathing and endless injustice.

The original binaries of Adam and Eve orchestrated that religious puritanical, sexist faith that endorsed the bigotry, adultery and the violence they all exposed to me at some time or other during my childhood.

Understanding, allowing and equalising all of that information was my first big step in fully rebuilding who I am. The instant I did, the freedom overwhelmed me. Feedback also exploded into my outside world as a beautiful stranger approached me and we conversed and he inform me he had just retired and now he was free to do whatever he wanted.

The second huge malfunction I had to rectify within me was my world's vocabulary of my body that was unjustified; I had to override that marketizing prejudice and view my female body as a magnificent piece of art.

With all my historical data and the uncovering of the continuous onslaughts from the outside world by cold hearted narcissistic authorities, who, even today, never take responsibility for their slanderous innuendos, with their boxed opinions of females and others in general, helped me realise why the reason behind my opinion of myself as so low grade.

The law of opposite and equal effect dealt me a blow when I realise it was because of centuries of **my** horrendous sexual discrimination against the female gender, that I was wearing that opinion as my garment. I was now literally living my accusations as they physically defined me as that woman.

It didn't matter whether I agreed or disagreed. The default program of the bad behaviour from my male attitude toward females was set in historical stone in my binary codes therefore my appearance.

Fighting or crusading against them only gave them more power and me the path of more injustice. I have to empower all of me now. I have to, from the inside out make me more visible again. I have to listen to me. I have to act and feel more my Eve, *the woman* I'm proud to represent, from the inside out.

But how does one achieve that when everywhere one looks, we, as humans, are competitively marketed as, "not quite good enough." Aah the world of capitalism, "keep them down."

They can remodel your physical flaws; they can heal your wounds; they can alter your appearance but only you can repair you. The financial narcissistic few will always maintain division, by playing one side against the other. By maintaining the constant imbalance, they maintain their wealth and power that way; first laws of narcissism.

If I want all my power back, my real power I have to first understand all that it isn't. Then I have to understand that I have always had it; now I have to allow it.

I have to mentally upgrade me to the woman I am proud to be; physically, mentally and, in my case, weirdly intellectually, then allow and empower all of them to amplify the magnificent beauty that I am.

No more fat or healthy; neither exist: No more empowering one side over the other. I blend all of me into one magnificent being and empower all of those magical emotions equally within me.

I have to reunite my voluptuous womanhood.

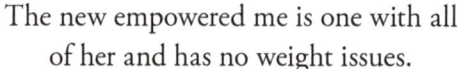

The new empowered me is one with all
of her and has no weight issues.

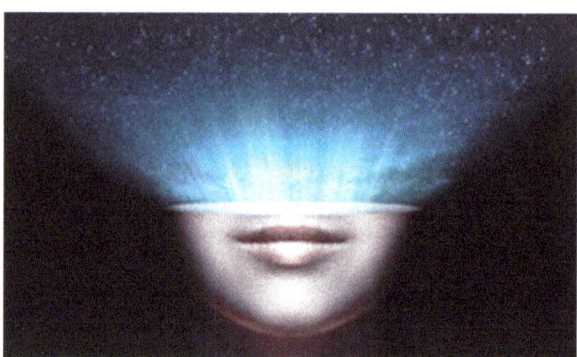

By finding and understanding my Eve, I treat everyone with respect and as an equal to all beings throughout the entire universes. I am now able to understand how I am truly equal to all things. These practices are my new allegiances, my new cornerstone, my saving grace, my oneness.

As an educated barbarian from the past, I also enforced the law that woman was soul-less, godless. But it was false. It was another narcissistic power play for the superior egocentric within me to divide nations, to divide me.

Now I know the God code is in every morsel of every cell of every living thing throughout the universe, we don't need a principle of some egocentric empty soul that was used as leverage to persecute.

The real soul is equivalent to every person's psyche, every animal's psyche for that matter, every living thing throughout the universe has it, even GI Joe; the pigeon who flew from Germany to England in WW2 and saved thousands of soldiers. It did that through its connection to its instinctual psyche or soul.

The soul is actively alive and in every morsel of every cell in every existing thing and much further. If you place cement on a wall and a piece chips off, then under a microscope you will find billions of moving cells. Those cells are exactly the same as your cells only now they are instrumentally concocted with toxins and water; but none of it could not exist without the original God code, it's impossible.

The other magical inference is; "I already have everything I desire and more. Don't ask."

This adage is our biggest misunderstanding. Because God is non-judgemental it allows you to walk your own path, your own way, knowing that if you make a mistake, there will be repercussions, however, it will also supply you with all the feedback necessary for you to rectify it, but it will not, cannot, do it for you. Everything is perfect; Everything is as it should be, there is never any need for any assistance.

When I say my God is oneness, I informing you it is all things equally, as one, undivided. It truly is the most momentous power in existence for it is all things equally and as such it allows all things equally. So, for me to achieve complete happiness I have to do the same. I have to learn to allow all the emotional injustices within me to be equal to the justices within me as one.

If you ask, you will experience all that it isn't. Then you react and the injustice continue.

My reactions were to my feelings of emotional injustices of the very jagged love I believed I was entitled to centuries ago. This unacceptable abuse was enforced by my bombastic bad behaviour from the narcissistic component of me both as male and female. I wore this as body of history for centuries.

My body has evolved this way, this time, due to all my pastlife emotional injustices, opinions, reactions and repercussions. With each indignation I mentally altered my genetic DNA and chromosomes to sculpture me in this manner, this way, this time. I live this garment of all those discriminating opinions. I wear all of them as evidence and feedback, even the bureaucratic opinions of the competitive marketeers. They are also informing me of my bombastic opinions

Acceptance is one thing; gratitude is another; but allowing is the gift of the Gods. I have to allow, that if it wasn't for all the bad behaviour exposed by the people around me in this existence, I would never have recognised the underlying contributors to all my personal anguish which is the cause of my ill health today.

Now it may be too late to alter my health issues today but, I can work with them and still have a long reasonably healthy life. Instead of empowering my victimising ill health, I can allow its existence with my amazing good health and appreciate them as one.

I can allow both forms of health to exist within me, empowering neither individually, but empowering both equally as one within me. The weakness of my ill health will determine the strength of my good health to equal value. They are the same. They are me.

EMPOWERING MY OPULENCE

When I first started seeing my therapist friend, she was much more than I expected. She informed me that many women of my age were having the same difficultly as me because according to her, we were caught in the cross fire of several generations at once.

> *We were told no; we were told yes; we were told*
> *go for it; but we had nowhere to go.*

When the American soldiers arrived in Australia and literally had their way with many of the girls, their government introduced the war brides act. The men could literally fornicate with anyone they liked without responsibility. They weren't bound to marry any of them and if they did, the marriage could be annulled at sea. Many Australian women were left with bastardised children.

The same thing occurred with Vietnam. These laws not only allowed Americanised recklessness, it almost enforced it. It allowed derogatory behaviour with the weaker sex of all races. It allowed abandonment of parental duties, it allowed abuse of opposite and same sex relationships under the guise of the supremist grandeur of war.

Then came the repercussions of that generation's capriciousness. Churches, politicians, families, all got in on the act of puritanical frigidness. What this meant was what Martin Luther said. "God says; Women are either wives or whores." So, the men married the wives and screwed the whores, and this was the new acceptable behavioural patterns of the sixties, seventies and eighties.

This two-faced attitude from society bewildered me even at that small age. How come the women were tagged with this discriminatory characterisation and men walked away unscathed without any responsibility for any of their actions. At that age I didn't realise this attitude had been a historical epitaph for over 20000 centuries.

So, when the sixties came, I can understand why women fought for equal rights. It became the age of free love, however, only the young partook of its sensationalism. No wonder my generation had a difficult time.

So many fractured rules and all of them completely ludicrous and my generation of women were torn in the middle. My country still remained abstinent and frigid in its allegiances to sex during this period but the men including the bishops, priests, teachers, politician and highly ranked business men, didn't and still don't.

These imprisoning beliefs systems were the cornerstone of our society. No wonder we hated ourselves, or reached for a god to save us; no human was going to.

This preposterous period rendered the very heart of a generation of young women. They struggled to become more than what they were only to be consistently put back into some dogmatic boxes to be quietened, again.

Women worked harder, raised families, kept homes, and still were subject to acts of atrocious physical and mental violence, and when we fell pregnant, we lost our jobs, and weren't allowed back into the work force till the children were 21. There was a no child care, no child support, no help anywhere, and usually a violent, drunken, philandering husband. We tried to fight, we tried to be seen and continually lost our battle, for another decade.

And buddha again proved to be right, "*for to fight outwardly was to give our power away to fools"* and that is what we did, till 1972-75. Then came the very small windowed timeline reprieve in our new brilliant prime minister, Gough Whitlam. This man opened doors for women, the poor, the workman and Australia. He gave us schooling and hospitalisation for the poor. He gave mothers an endowment to return to work and pay for a babysitter. His slogan "time for a change," took a country suffering from immortal despotism and gave them the key to freedom and equality for a brief period.

He saw his country as one, equal and something the world would have to contend with. He gave our sporting youth the AIS, an institution to be trained with the best the country had to offer. Then a narcissistic liberal government destroyed a high percentage of it, for according to them, it destroyed their narcissistic capitalism. The wealthy would suffer at the hands of equality. Then they proved their worth by their cowardly actions of betrayal of a nation and proved the path of liberal narcissism in history.

IF SOMEONE IS TRYING TO MAKE YOU SMALL,

IT ONLY MEANS ONE THING,

YOU WERE ALREADY BIGGER THAN THEM.

With this new found freedom my objective now was to empower me, the woman and not worry about the outside capitalistic world.

That was where my true problem was. According to the world I needed the material things to survive. I needed to work so many hours per week to get paid. I needed to earn so much money per week to pay my rent. I needed to have sufficient money to buy my stuff. According to capitalism you have to have the money, even if it is a loan, before you can have the dream.

This assessment of my life and existence dictated that all these material things of the world would determine my acceptance by the world standards. In my comparison of me to the world, I had to look at my innermost fear. I had to deal with my relationship with poverty according to the opinions of the five percent with the wealth.

My true innermost doubt was exposing my opinion of my material lack and this was dictating my lifestyle according to the capitalistic world. Then that lifestyle crushed me to extinction and detrimental ill health.

This is the law of Nirvana. The material world can only supply emptiness. What you echo; you receive.

My outside world cannot provide me with what I truly need. It can only provide me with a false sense of security, a false sense of achievement, when in fact it is literally demeaning and abusing me. Only I can provide me with what I truly need.

Capitalism; they own 95% of the wealth you have 5% of the wealth You need the money to have the dream.

Entrepreneurs have the dream, then the money comes to them. 100% of it. The money determines the size of your dream. You want more money,

DREAM BIGGER.

Bill Gates, Walt Disney, are only two that I will mention. You have a dream. Share it with everyone equally. Why? Because everyone on earth is equal to you. You are treating them equally and thus fulfilling their dreams also.

Make your feeling of your dream something you can take with you from life time to life time. Allow it to expand here in this life time and watch it grow. By watching how your wealth expands, you can determine how to expand your dream.

Your wealth is only your reward card, expressing the feedback of the value of your dreams, not the other way around. If your dream is money and taking it from others to make you wealthy, then also imagine the dream of immense impoverishment and poverty for this also is your future path of opposite and equalised value.

LET YOUR DREAMS FLOW THROUGH YOU;
LET YOU DREAMS GUIDE YOUR WAY;
BE YOUR DREAMS EVERY DAY.

TAKE CARE OF YOU FIRST

I AM MY KEEPER

NOW CAN YOU SEE ME?

Chapter Twelve

AVANT-GARDE ME

NOW SEE ME

Imagine standing in front of you is a giant replica of you and all your cells are small miniature pieces of Lego. They all look alike; they all contain the same information of all the universe. The embodiment looks exactly like you with the colouring for the eyes, hair, lips and body. It's almost as if you are looking in a mirror.

Every component of your body has been considered. All of it is now comprised of miniscule Lego pieces; your organs, your muscles your sinews your blood.

In your hand, you hold one singular piece. Just one single piece of Lego, any colour your like. It may be coloured, clear, crystal or plastic.

This duplication is an embodiment of you in your physical state. Every single piece represents some past emotional attitude within you. Your visual sculpture of all your centuries of evolution.

Body of History

Look at it, examine it, admire it, be pleased with your evolutionary construction. This is how you evolved from monkey to man; from Adam to nuclear man.

This is who you evolved into. You are the physical evolution of every nano emotion that exists within you.

Now get a bat, a tractor, acid, whatever it takes to smash it to the ground and vaporise it completely. Distinguish it, annihilate it, dissolve it into nothing. Dissolve the floor that holds it, the walls that conceal it, the ceiling that covers and protects it, all that had it enclosed until you see nothing but emptiness and darkness. Nothing of it exists except the one piece you hold in your hand.

This represents the original single cell creature in the water of the earth for zillions of years before life on earth, before we ventured on land. It evolved and like its environment developed instincts. An emotional struggle to survive. It divided and duplicated, then did it again and again and again

Two cell, four cell, eight cells; after billions of years of evolution, this newly developed water creature ventured to land and became man. His need to survive attitude was already a strong component of his personality. This is our original binary code. You are holding it in your hand.

Now look at it. How does it feel? See it for what it truly was. The keystone of your pastlife perceptions of your old beliefs, philosophies, histories, existences that have bought you to this moment in time. This small piece of Lego is responsible for all the wars, impoverishment, vandalism of the earth, desecration of human kind, everything around you to this day, revealing to you what everything isn't.

Explaining why you exist this way. Brandishing your constant need to question, to pray, to ask why. Exposing your ongoing emotional need to experience all there is to know about all the injustices that exist.

Now throw it away. Throw it as far away from you as you possibly can, never to see hide nor hair of it again.

That was the cornerstone of all Adam's and Eve's ego centred anarchy throughout history to today. It was the instinctual egocentric emotional binary of every being that is responsible for the underlying victimising attitudes of the world as it stands today. We can't alter the past but we can allow it, we can understand it.

Now what stands before you? NOTHINGNESS, darkness. There is nothing around but the empty silence of black. It is weightless, thoughtless, noiseless, emotionless, feelingless, perfectly still.

Now you have a clean slate; the opportunity to create the life you truly wish to experience. Within that nothingness is everything we need to recreate the new YOU and the existences you now wish to experience.

You can give you all the health wealth and happiness beyond your imagination. You can create experiences to fulfill your highest imaginings. You can provide yourself with more happiness than you ever thought possible. This is all yours now. This is your future life; this is your Nirvana.

In order to understand all that Nirvana is; You have to experience all that Nirvana isn't.

Now the penny drops. You've done this before; thousands and thousands of times. This is the reincarnational continuum. This is history repeating itself.

Every existence, you upgrade, expand, evolve but you are continually walking the path of Nirvana until you reach the path or realisation and start again. You have developed from a single cell amoeba to a narcissistic war machine to understand Nirvana.

Lesson number one; you really did supply you with everything you will ever need to have the most amazing existence, so, learn to allow yourself to have your all hearts desires; "Don't ask!"

Allow the universe to provide. "ask and you **will** receive," and you will receive "all that it isn't," because you are asking from the psyche of victim. You will then endure all there is to experience until you choose to no longer be victim.

One of the biggest curfews that occurs when I speak at seminars to small groups incorporating men is their inability to realise that I'm not sexist nor a women's liberationist, I'm simply the messenger.

When I re-educate them on history which is part of my program, I have to expose the bias and bigotry portrayed by the egocentric narcissistic supremist attitude of Adam and the constant victimising embodiment of EVE what she had to endure as his enabler. I inform them of how his mind-set manipulated history to portray males as heroes, when in truth they purveyed man at his worst, as cold-hearted murdering materialistic cowards.

The other major obstacle that has only recently been overcome since 1970 is now women can re-write their history. Natives can re-write their history; subjugated others can tell their stories and they are.

We can alter all the old prehistoric canards and reveal a better option. For the facts are "Everything is Absolutely Perfect;" We are now being offered insights that reveal the real truth.

Yang man is believed to be the light and Yin woman believed to be the darkness. However, in the contrivance for power and greed, these principles have been manipulated by hierarchy to create extreme unjustified segregation through control of others.

As with the words "love" and "hate" that truly do not exist but are simply a state of mind; the same code exists with Yin/Yang and ADAM/EVE. They are not people per sae; they are emotional states of actuality.

Since I discovered the paths of the reincarnational continuum in 2012, I uncovered the contrivances that were manipulated by the few to acquire those chosen paths of power.

Through further study I also revealed that by comprehending the "power of oneness," then by using the tools of allowance, we are capable of altering all future lives equally to attain a better future for all.

Let's start rebuilding us from scratch.

What will you use this time? Crystals? Stars? Diamonds? Or will you stick to Lego only more colourful more powerful. Gold, silver, quartz? This is the new you. You can now choose anything you want.

The first brick is your future psyche. We are no longer in victim survival mode. We have evolved. We no longer have to kill or be killed.

Your new basic psyche has to be one of oneness of all things; equality for all. If it wasn't for the heinous path Adam paved, I would not understand the path of justice, equality, self-empowerment, self-love. Every monstrous result of Adam's path lays before me on display in my outer world, and without any one of them, I could never know Eve. My new psyche, must be equal, level, undivided. Eve and Adam united. That's my new cornerstone block.

I allow Adam; I allow Eve; There paths of victimisation were and still are allowed; I simply choose not to follow. This alters my psyche to one of allowance.

Next, for me to stand in front of a mirror and tell myself I loved me was not going to work for me at this stage, not after sixty odd years of feeling quite the opposite. I had to find ways to improve what I actually saw.

The revelation that all the dissatisfaction I saw reflected in my mirror was revealing all my true inner beauty; I wasn't there yet either.

I had this inner desire to alter my interpretation of what I saw. Now did this feeling mean diets and exercise? No. It meant allowing me to experience genuine manners to love me as I saw myself now.

If I started an alteration campaign, I had to be careful I wasn't judging myself and empowering one injustice component of me over another. I had to learn to love all of me as I am now and empower all of me now equally, then allow the universe to introduce me to my Eve.

I knew what she felt like; I didn't know how she looked. My outside world was still revealing my world of Adam.

My therapist friend suggested, as an experiment, I should start with underwear. When you are size "BIG," underwear, undergarments are not essential as much as a necessity.

I had never indulged in anything sexy or salacious for my body ever, because I never believed my body to be sexy enough to warrant it, from the age of puberty.

It felt almost risqué. I wore my usual boring attire over the top, so that I was the only one who knew what was hidden underneath. My outer world results were quite rapid, unexpected and weird.

Although I inwardly perceived myself to feel sexy, for me, and I was doing this entire exercise for me; I didn't think I'd echo that feeling of inner ecstasy to my outside world; but apparently, I did.

This revelation informed me that although I personally cannot empower another human being, my binaries do reverberate with others who binaries match. By empowering me in one form or another and rearranging my algorithms into binaries of personal self-empowerment, I matched with others with the similar attitudes.

Apparently as with the law of attraction we are able to tickle the ivories in your outer world so others who are experiencing the same attitudes are attracted to us. This also explained the enabler connection between Adam and Eve.

What my experiment also revealed was; we were all re-living a past timeline, doing this same exercise with the same impact only from the opposite perspective. No, I don't personally empower others. But, without raising a finger, I am able to, from inside of me, alter my outside environment of people places and things to comply with my new attitude of me, instantaneously.

When buddha states; "your inner thoughts words and actions echo your outer world," this is what it means.

I'm usually a recluse; I hide; people don't talk to me. I live in silence. I was invisible to the world. Well almost.

My daughter informs me I have a serious problem. I talk to myself all the time; and I do.

All of a sudden, strangers started talking to me as I walked to my car or sat quietly waiting for my coffee. I received a flower from a stranger, who thought I was nice. I received an invitation to dinner from a stranger who heard me singing to myself.

My new form of self-confidence motivated me to experiment more. I then had my hair cut and styled; then even weirder invitations started coming out of the woodworks. This little experiment now switched to research as well as fun.

My inner self-assurance as a more confident woman was echoing to my outer world but other than altering my perception of my appearance, I was doing nothing. I appeared to have become visible.

I was appreciating myself as a woman more and enhancing my personal value of me. Now my outside world was appreciating me as the equalised voluptuous woman I felt I was now portraying in my mirror.

This feedback excited me so I began developing more intense variations of the new woman I wanted to expose to my outer world.

When my daughter came to assist me after an operation went severely awry, we decluttered much of my old wardrobe, now there was room for improvement, however, I still hadn't envisaged the complete story of the new me I wanted to be.

I am still a work in progress; however, what I do know and can verify is;

> *When you empower you and not your outside world;*
> *you empower you in your outside world.*

To me, my alteration began by having the courage to tell myself that the God the narcissistic Adam was offering me with its terms and conditions was not suitable for me, and I wanted one that would support me first and foremost as a woman, then as woman without a man, a woman who is not a man's possession, as Napoleon stated. I allowed this emotional freedom of choice to come to me for it gave me the passage to the God I wanted. A God that gave me the inner support I needed to stand alone, yet not alone and not be classed as some whore, but as a vibrant voluptuous woman.

With my inner God, I am liberated, I am a new breed of Eve and Adam. As this woman I am allowed to stand alone or be with a partner should I choose either.

I am equalised within me. Instead of being divided, denigrated and slandered as a slut and a whore, and struggling against the injustice because I'm single. I'm allowed to be a complete woman and not be used as partisan for the personal sexual satisfaction or barbie presentation of some narcissistic macho marketeer.

As this new empowered and balanced Eve, I am allowed to be educated. I am allowed to show and display my intelligence without being informed that if that is the case there is something wrong with my sexual organs.

As Eve I am allowed to understand equal rights for all. It does not make me a witch, who will murder my children, destroys my marriage, becomes a lesbian, or ruin capitalism.

As Eve I am allowed to enjoy having sex with a partner without wanting to have children. It is not going to deem me to a hell, but I can experience a sensual ***love*** in its highest formulation of exhilaration. I'm allowed that experience for I'm not asking. I'm no longer a reflection of some vicitmised narcissistic devil or demon

As Eve, my actions although rebellious to many, freed me from the barbaric puritanical narcissistic binds of my predecessors and gave me more than I could ever hope for. It gave me my Eve. It gave me back to ME as an equalised, self- empowered, voluptuous woman.

Yes, I am ALL woman and I allow all of her. I have curves. I have breasts. I have a tummy with stretchmarks where I have had babies. I have hips. I have thighs. I have more rolls than the baker's dozen, in fact I have more rolls than the entire bakery.

I have white hair now where it used to be copper. I wear glasses for driving, glasses for reading the computer, glasses for writing my books and glasses for the sun.

I'm aged and wrinkled. I have for more chins than I need and have more medication than the pharmacist. I take medication for the medication.

The medication has side effects and that warrants more medication. I rattle when I walk. I have a choice; medication and breathe and live longer or no medication and suffer the consequences. This is all of me. This is who my Eve is.

This was my father's path; this was my mother's path, meaning I lived this ill health timeline in my past and am reliving it now, so understanding and allowance is more essential as opposed to fighting it.

It took me a long while to get here, centuries in fact. My paths were arduous and it has taken its toll on me physically. I have to walk every day to strengthen my lungs so I can breathe. I have to watch what goes into my mouth as my medication automatically puts weight on me. I cannot go out into the sun, cannot dance, sing or physically exert myself.

To appreciate my good health, I had to experience ill health. I gave myself good health so now I claim it and allow it. So, I am my strong person with my sick person; I do what I can without exerting myself. I dance to a verse of a song instead of an entire song. I sing in a lower register now, and instead of walking for 10 klms per day I walk for 6 min three times a day.

I empower my health, all of it and give it a new name "well-being." I empower my energy to strengthen all of me, now, equally. I am not ill health nor good health, I'm both.

I also have some wonderful clients and several genuine new friends now. 10% of my family treat me with respect I want, for they now appreciate that I will no longer be victim and allow them to put me in their diabolical little boxes. Oh, they still do not understand anything of what I'm talking about, but that's okay.

I know nothing of football, cricket golf or fishing either. We are equal. That is allowed.

I have amazing support from a magnificent daughter and son-in- law that are above reproach. I still have my awesome son who has always allowed me to be me. He amazes me, for he always saw more. They mirror me. They reveal my inner courage and happiness. I know I can be more. It's up to me.

More than anything else now, I have ME. An amazing voluptuous equalised Eve who smiles all the time. I don't need the supposed love of others as vicitmised crutches determine from injustice.

I allow them to love me their way. Some do; some don't; but without their pettiness I could never understand the obscurities of the emotional injustices of what love isn't. I needed to understand that so I could appreciate a love that is within me filled with the most magnificent possibilities.

That's what I had to learn. This is what I have learnt. To understand all that self-empowerment and self-love is, I had to experience all that it wasn't.

Now I am no longer invisible to my outside world. I'm also visible inside as well. I'm alive, happy and kickin' butt. I am no longer size 22 but I'm not size 6 either.

The outside world is allowed to love and judge me their way but, if I want to be loved my way, I have to be the one to do it first.

MY next building block is my allowance for me to accept all the gifts I supplied for me in my Nirvana state of bliss. My blossoming gifts for my new Avant Garde Me. The understanding that I can now rebuild me as the real woman I am. A magnificent woman I love and appreciate in all ways equally.

Now like my grand-daughter, I can be whoever I want; do whatever I want; go where ever I want. Like my grand-daughter,

I'd rather be a sparrow than a snail.

You are not here for anybody else; you can only be good to yourself; that's self-empowerment.

Body of History

You cannot do for others; you cannot save them;

*And you cannot love them; you can only love
  yourself: they have to love themselves.*

You are not your brother's keeper; they are.

*By you displaying self-empowerment you can provide them with
an optional choice to follow, but you cannot do it for them.*

*We need to forget who we think we are;
So, we can become who we really are:*

Paulo Coelho.

FINDING THE LOVE OF MY LIVES

There's an old gypsy adage that says,

"You *may marry many times, but you love only once.*"

In my book The Prophet I explain this by having the heroine experience several past life regressions. She and her soul mate get distracted by other paths and although they are soul bound, they are separated through many life experiences for 1900 years.

After sixty odd years of this austere perception of the non-love and I'm saying non-love because in reality from every perspective the love that surrounded me was from the victimised stance. It was re-produced from my past karmic timelines of low self-esteem and slavery. I knew no other type of love. I never saw it; I was never shown it; and no one loved me enough to show me how to experience in any other way. So, I could not complain, for the information was not available. No one knew any better.

This unresponsive love had me being my brother's helper or keeper when they were in need, for to encourage them to stand on their own two feet was considered selfish, thoughtless, uncharitable, unkind, even lazy.

I believed I was not that kind of uncharitable person so I bent over backwards at the cost of my own health to prove that I was a nice invaluable person. Unbeknownst to them, they reacted, and then we all proceeded to re-live the repercussions of old timelines. Now people walked all over me and crushed me into the same toxic fertilised compost heap of victimisation I displayed in my past life.

When your entire perception of love has been based on that noxious form of emotional blackmail, manipulation and extortion from others, it was difficult for me to discern fact from fiction.

When I finally confronted the futility of this entire situation it was a massive reality check. What I had to discern was, none of this experience was love; not the love I truly wanted, but it was the love I was projecting; the reactions I created. Then the ultimate question had to be asked. What kind of love did I want if the love I was getting wasn't the love I wanted? Historically I was shown.

Pondering this poser many abhorrent answers from past historical incriminations came to mind of what I didn't want. But I had never encountered any form of the real love that I truly wanted to experience. I didn't know what to ask for.

Saint Odelion, describes women as an abomination, bile of humours, excrement, vomit, and shit. Montagne states sex with a woman is like shitting in a bucket and tipping it on your head. Martin Luther says, we are either wives or whores. Confucius says one hundred women aren't worth one man's testicle.

These men were pious chaste men, saints under the christian churches protection. This is their mandate, their man-made God beliefs. This is their allegiances. No wonder men only appreciate football, meat pies, and fast cars and atomic warfare.

For centuries, their binaries too have been matched with liars and deceitful doctrines from the emotionally unjust materialistic perception of love also. They were uneducated too. They determined their conclusions from their own personal realities. Their teachers were the greedy powerful lustful leaders, kings and popes who knew power, but nothing of love.

The true oneness allows the narcissistic values of men to be obnoxious bores understanding that these evaluations do in fact reveal what true love is. These arrogant boorish masters were demonstrating what love isn't. They displayed how by using the intensity of subjugation, they achieved the most awe-inspiring results of karma in opposite and equal value.

This knowledge revealed that without that entire experience for over 200000 years, I would not understand its opposite and equal value of love.

Without every immoral desecration I would never be able to embrace and encompass the passions and desires that real love can aspire to; then allow them to empower and equalise all of me to my highest potential.

This is the oneness of love. This is the love of the oneness. You cannot have one without the other. This is the love I wanted me to aspire to and now I know what it isn't; so, that means, I also know what it is.

All this time, for centuries, as a victimised Eve I have taken the brunt of the blame for man's bad behaviour. The pristine scribes may have taught the truth, but ambitious uneducated narcissistic leaders of men manipulated these teachings and dictated their abhorrence as a means to acquire all that isn't love; personal material wealth and greed. As a result, as an uneducated enabler I accepted their crumbs and handouts and grovelled, assuming it to be love.

By re-examining all the information before me, it was as if I was unfolding a huge mathematical equation of all my existences across time and space.

I was re-living my emotional triggers over and over again to past life judgements from the different perspectives of injustice. The more I reacted, the bigger and more intense those assumptions embodied me; It was all inner feelings and outer attitude, just like the lovely underwear. The more I felt good about myself the more my world reflected how I felt and responded.

In this case, the more I rejected myself the more I reflected that to my outer world; the more intensely the outer world reacted to me. Regardless of the "justice or injustice" I demonstrated or the argument of "for or against," the underlying psyche of me was victimised injustice.

BODY OF HISTORY

The phraseology that a picture is worth 1000 words, in this case is invaluable. Try this exercise.

For two seconds focus on each suggestion.

Man drowning at sea.

Birth of a baby.

Child winning race at sports event.

Wedding, funeral, birthday.

We are capable of instantly creating an entire movie length synopsis with one thought in the miniscule of a second. Now add some emotional pain or joy to that memory and that enhances that image. However, they are only images or imaginative situations, but you created them from nothing.

This unfortunately is our magic wand. The reason I say unfortunate is because we don't know how to use it correctly. We thrust it around willy-nilly, come up with utter chaos then blame some poor imaginary God, with the hope it will now save you. Without knowing it, you are inadvertently asking, now you will receive all that it isn't.

By understanding oneness, we realise we already have more than what we need. Our supercilious need for love may only be one of the amazing emancipations prepared for you. By asking you restrict your possibilities.

I know that with every thought and reaction I alter my binary; by allowing, I still alter my binaries, but now they read what I want it to experience, as opposed to what I've react to.

I no longer have to plead for forgiveness or beg to be saved, for I know I have already been saved. I use my new breed Eve and Adam power to create my new story perfectly, equally and if it is unsuitable then the challenge is within me.

The people around me will give me feedback through their words, thoughts, and actions as to the vicitmised progress of what my attitude patterns are revealing. Their binaries match mine. By listening I can remain victim or choose another path.

I realise we are re-living a past timeline of an old emotions. I realise I am proficient with that emotion and know how it ends. I allow it to exist, within me, now I am creating a better attitude a more reliable one to replace my victimised one.

N.B. You can only alter past life indiscretions as they arise, and they will arise. However now knowing they will arise you have the tools to respond as opposed to react.

History teaches us that according to man and society, as a woman, I was an abomination, but as an obese woman, today; I am repugnant.

I'm still over weight according to social standards, for I do not look like the skinny 12-year-old waif.

However, to be that statuesque woman I have to exist in their world. The competitive dispirited, cold, vain materialistic world of emotional injustices and division. I've been there; I've experienced that and I know where it ends; powerlessness and victimisation.

My new voluptuous woman code is, I'm a fully developed woman, with all the essential resplendence and more. I am not just Eve female only. I'm the turbo charged, fully self-empowered, self-loving, embodiment of womanhood who is both Eve and Adam evolved.

Yes, I am not skin and bone, but I'm a magnificent specimen of womanhood who has suffered physically, mentally, financially and intellectually through the hands of some barbaric male and female specimens who assumed precedence because of some emotional injustice I ensued. They were only the tools.

I know their actions were unacceptable behaviour, but in allowing them to remain as they are without judgement, I am able to use their feedback as stronger stepping stones for me to gain to a higher more acceptable perspective of me.

In experiencing what love isn't I am able to understand what love is. I understand you cannot have one without the other. They are both within us at all times. However, it is our constant feelings of injustice to specific situations that keeps empowering it to a higher and more evolved experience.

By learning to respond naturally continuously, as opposed to react, we automatically manifest from our more productive attitude without thinking.

When I do eventually find the love of my life, either in this life or the next, I will be the amazing self-empowered woman I am for I have experienced many lives as a powerless female victim of circumstances and I know what that is.

I will not go to hell; I will not burn; but what this equalisation will do for me is; when I die, the emotional empowering exhilaration I feel within me will alter my binaries and my DNA. It will alter my chromosomes to the Eve who is no longer a victim to oppressive obscene vulgarity. My binaries will match a world of equalised love as well. I'll evolve into a being of true magnificent oneness with ingenuity and initiative. That's a woman worth coming back to.

I embody Eve within me now. I will experience relationships with boundless sexual joy and empowerment and it will go with me into the next life so I can match it with synchronised binary and find love again.

My love and I will have most amazing sensual love and appreciation in each existence for our binaries will match and we will allow the gifts that we created for us to enjoy to flourish through us. Instead of the high volatile waves of karma; a flat timeline where I may still observe the denigration of women but choose not to participate in it. I now know how to equalise it, balance it. That's a timeline worth creating.

My genes and chromosomes will start embodying me now as this new evolved woman. The next generation already had their chromosomes altered when they arrived here. That's why they are my future. That's why women are able to stand up now.

The united front of man and woman together. A united front of the intellectuals, the empowered, loving, the magnificent, are all comprised component of me, beautifully; equally, adoringly.

My love's binaries and mine will treat each other lovingly and equally with the physical, mental and the intellectual respect we deserve. We have to all be on the same page. I have always stated that the man who marries someone like me has to be intellectually mad.

Mad as in Van Gogh. His work was insightful, ahead of his time. It was brilliant and emotionally intuitive but he couldn't buy a loaf of bread for it. Now today he could buy every bakery in the world and still have enough change for all the coffee shops as well.

Einstein is quoted as saying; "an intelligent conversation is an extremely sensual experience." I am yet to have that experience but to have an intellectually sensual relationship is definitely on my bucket list.

So, from these deductions, I know I would have allowed me to have them to experience. These are the things I'd love to have in my life, the way I want them so I know I have them. I no longer put numbers or time on them. I allow them to come when they are ready. I'm not to be sized at 10, 12, 18 for that creates limitations and divisions. I've already experienced that and I know where it ends. I already am who I'm supposed to be to experience all the joys that I have provided for me, they are coming to me without question. I now have to live it.

The shape I expose will dictate the woman within. The woman within will echo who I am to the world. I am a self-empowered, self-loving, voluptuous amorous woman whatever size I am. That's my perception of me as a woman. That's my attitude, my embodiment, my Eve.

My new story for me is unfolding for me physically, emotionally, sexually and intellectually every second of every day.

I love my shape and every intricate part of me with all my heart.

I lived all those horrendous existences and they are my body of history but without one of them I would not be here now. Every single intricate part was vital to my evolution. I respect the pain I had to endure to get me here for without it I would not understand the true meaning of justice, equality, self-love and self-empowerment.

I now stand and speak for equal options for the new generations and those who are older; who have had enough unacceptable abuse; who were never given another option.

I speak for those who wanted a God in their life who genuinely has their back as opposed to one who genuinely stabbed them in the back.

A God who reunites you as one. It does not presume power over you; that is injustice. To say God is love is to say hate is the devil. God is both, we are both, now learn how to empower them all as one.

THAT'S EQUALITY; THAT'S EMPOWERMENT:

Oneness gives you options, offering resolutions to unrelenting pain that needs to exist, but not necessarily be experienced.

Options that allow you to recognise that specific paths are predestined time lines and if you want out you can take it, instead of being in default mode and following through to a future that you really do not wish to par-take in.

What's more, there is resolute proof behind these theories whereas the narcissistic male's false God's high falootin,' airy fairy belief possibilities leave you high and dry without an answer, sitting on a cloud.

What I'm sharing is expressions of variable options on how to allow happiness within yourself.

I leave these options on the table and I walk away.

I walk away; for if you do not like them, rather than fighting and arguing with me to prove their definite formation, you too are allowed to let them go. This is equality in action. This is my next component of my Avant Garde Lego; ALLOWANCE.

I respect you enough to allow you to choose your own path. All I ask is that you do the same for me. In doing that, you too have created equality within you.

NOW I NOT ONLY SEE WHO I CAN POSSIBLY BE;
I'M AM THE ME I TRULY WANT TO BE.

AVANT-GARDE ME

NOW CAN YOU SEE ME?

Chapter Thirteen

I WAS VICTIM.

NOW SEE ME

All the unacceptable denigration and humiliation imposed upon us as women was from victim mode. We reacted to the emotional injustice imposed upon us thus subjecting us to more and more and more. Lack of education was another one of those paths.

It is by experiencing what wisdom isn't;
That you understand what true acumen is.

Through our emotional judgement women constantly subjected themselves to endure atrocious behaviour and ongoing obliviousness, thus, being deceived of what was really happening to us due to our ignorance?

As I said, as a child, I was not overly educated due to the codes of our existence. It wasn't because I wouldn't understand it, it was because it was never available.

This is why we had to endure those prejudiced ongoing laws and edicts. We reacted, we created, and as a result have had to suffer intense ongoing violence, abuse and chaos in both private and worldly sectors, that could have all been resolved honestly and peacefully?

Billions of unnecessary deaths were tyrannized due to immoral fallacies. The authorities of churches and monarchy alike withheld the truth because they were only interested in their own ambitious wellbeing of money and power. No truthful research was ever entered into and even if it was, should the outcome be detrimental to the revenue of the hierarchy, it was over turned and deemed as blasphemous, occultism or mysticism.

For if they didn't ignore it, they would have had to relinquish their control of the people, the power and the wealth to a belief system of equality and freedom. They could never let that happen, for this was what they truly loved.

This action has been proven over and over again with Samos, Aristotle, Copernicus, Galileo who saw the light and the truth, but were rejected and imprisoned. Even Darwin reneged on his theories but was rejected

That's possibly why all forms of resistances other than their foolish ideology were always condoned as heresy, "in league with some dastardly devil," satanic, occult, when in fact, the very doctrines they brandished were brainwashing's with the exact same impact.

By exacerbating the strong dictatorship, the leaders created, with the matched fear of the enabling peoples, they were able to manipulate a new emotional fear of God principle deeming them to a hell and eternal damnation, or giving them a get out of jail free card by telling them they will automatically go to heaven. The feelings of the worshipers would always support the papal hierarchy matching the fear orientated dread. This binary was the path of emotional blackmail, victimisation and emotional injustice.

Not only doesn't their narcissistic God exist on a puffy cloud, neither does their narcissistic devil, Satan or hell. These diabolical or hellish assumptions were created out of fear by men to rule with an iron fist. To this day many treacherous politicians win elections utilising the same dreaded tactics and succeed.

So, in truth, it was our fear induce reactions to their terror orientated religious dogmas that are blackmailing us. This male egocentric human perception of their fear is represented in all the garments of the cruel dictatorial Gods and demonic devils they created.

This fear reverts back to our Adam's omnipotence again. By placing dread into their enemy's hearts, stealing their children, forcing them into slavery, then as they developed sexually assaulting them because they were their property, they were able to control them and victimise them.

This all-empowering fear is what gives these imaginary deities power over you. You then submit by becoming victim to these imaginary friends, relenting all your control.

But you are not giving up your power to your God, you are empowering your emotional injustice within you. You are empowering one emotion over the other; you are empowering your fear. You then matched the victim mode of some papal hierarchy fear who then used imaginary friends, whom you now perceive will hurt or destroy you if you don't submit.

The churches, monarchs, empires, leaders of the world, financial leaders, refuse to allow the real facts to be known. Emotional injustice is fear. Fear induces more obedient followers than any other emotional reaction. Everything else is a conspiracy. It has worked for over 20000 centuries, why would they change it now?

During Egyptian times, the high priests would hire engineers to create awe inspiring trickery within their temples to stage-manage their worshippers into fear.

So, when a church elder, whom you believed to be in cahoots with some God, told you some cockamamie story that their God has communicated to them that there is a heaven and a hell and if you are good according to male standards you will go to heaven and if you are an abomination, you according to male standards you will go to some hell.

Of course, the uneducated, out of pure unadulterated fear will naturally believe. But by today's standards, if we educated our children that way, with those mind games without proof, it is classed as mental abuse.

Today, through hypnotherapy from anti indoctrinated clients, there is proof that neither place exists. They only live and exist in the consciousness of the mind of the believer.

Through constant brainwashing and emotional blackmail young children were programmed to visually see this indoctrination of hell. We all knew what Satin, this horned beast looked like and we all had a graphic fiery impression of what hell appeared like. With these fear mongering images unprincipled leaders bullied the young children into christian doctrinated fear.

Through religious brain washing, this fear tactic undermined children's old beliefs of freedom and happiness and provided them with an indoctrinated future fed on fear-dreaded lies.

If you choose to do that now, you can, but we as women are now allowing education and understand that through your declaration of fear, you only experience more fear, but from the opposite and equal perspective; meaning, in your next life you will be the one destroying the freedom of a child. However, if none of it exists until you create it, why create it?

> *You have to experience all the emotional injustices of victimisation to understand true freedom.*

The religious faction is like all other arenas, it is simply a field to express spiritual fears of injustice through victimisation.

If you could understand that fear, then learn to allow joy and exultation in to your life, wouldn't you rather alter your attitude to a better one, a more productive one?

> The reason I say productive is an old quote of "there will be poor always," should actually translate as, *"if you are cruel, unjust, and selfish, you will always be poor."*

What would incur from that adage is elders would translate it for this lifetime only. But with all spiritual inscription there is always a deeper more meaningful translation. It transcribes correctly as

"If you are cruel, unjust and selfish in this life, you will through these empty desires, create a poor life for you to experience in your next life."

There will be poor always, because the empty powerful materialistic promises create further emptiness to experience over and over again. Your lives are ongoing, you cannot take the material things with you, they are empty records of your existence.

If the elders of yore understood that; if they genuinely listened to what the American Indians and Australian Aborigines were teaching them, do you think the world would be in a better state?

Because the cold-hearted dictating leaders keep re-living their hedonistic lifetimes of greedy materialism, it is also with this overly ambitious avarice of this emptiness that they keep re-creating over and over to experience in their future immortal lives, so,

> There will be "poor" always.

Due to past life regressions and the research where the divided cell after being cut in half kept returning in its original condition and understanding we are nothing more than billions of cells, then the evidence deduces that even when we are cut in half we will return whole again. Many a victim of past wars who lost ligaments returned brand new. Some even flinched in areas where wounds had occurred in a past life.

We keep returning regardless of how we die. We are made up of zillions of immortal cells. The elders of yore made carbuncle up, not because they didn't believe in immortality; they simply didn't understand it.

They judged, juried, assumed and came up with the erroneous conclusions adapted from their worldly perceptions; unfortunately, now you have to carry many a ludicrous man-made falsehood that is unnecessary.

There is no mortal sin, nor is there venial sin. Everything is perfectly balanced so persecution was a choice, not a necessity. They are simply emotional paths imprinted on your psyche by your past life teachers.

Supposed answers created by their reactions to specific situation. You will not go to hell unless you create some form of illusionary hell for you to experience and yes, horrendous wars prove that path is very possible.

For example; we have been taught that suicide is the end of the path for all of us, it is a mortal sin it is wrong, evil and that ethos is all incorrect. What if I was to inform you, it is a new beginning for that being.

Once a suicide victim has taken their own life, the last component of that timeline is complete. They now need to embark on their new one. They then quickly return within a short period to begin their real mission in another new body usually due in the short interim.

Unlike the cot death or natural death of a child, the suicide victim does not necessarily return to the same lineage.

Once the suicide victim's mission is complete, their slate is cleaned; Many now return to re-join their true love. The love from the previous journey they were experiencing before they became distracted by this short-term suicide interim. They can now re-join that original timeline experience or start a completely new venture.

Because all timelines upgrade the suicide victim's binaries no longer match the old binaries so they too need to upgrade. To achieve this, they become miscarriages or cot deaths to update their binary to continue their original journey on that timeline.

These beings are often recognised in many different ways but one very obvious sign is when they marry or have continued relationships with people or lovers who are usually considerably older than they are.

This scenario always indicated to me that they were late. They had to fix something up first, then catchup to their real life that they wanted to live. This may take fifteen to twenty years.

Through our research of suicides, this was where we discovered the very stringent timelines of same age, same time, same place, same impact.

The fifteen-year-old child victim who takes their life this time, is the same age as the suicide victim they judged or expressed an opinion of in their past existence

The feeling of the emotional injustice caused to both parties at the time of the discriminatory act in the past, is exactly the same excruciating pain caused to the participant at the time of the suicide in this life.

The question asked is actual unjustified pain, the feeling, the unjust agony is the underlying victimising emotional injustice paving this path of suicide. It is informing the inquirer that this is another form of hopeless victimisation of injustice for you to experience. The despairing impact of this particular form of emotion always results in suicide.

The is the journey of the suicide alone. It is indicated by this type of pain only. Should anyone choose to experience this type of pain, this is how it performs.

Now you know how this emotional injustice of hopelessness works; you know how it ends. This experience was for you to understand empowerment.

How can that possibly be a mortal sin?

NEW SOULS as they were called are the most misinterpreted of all beings. The only thing that is new is the chromosome, and we do that for every new evolution. Suicide victims become the new souls.

A new being re-appears when a slate has been wiped clean and there are no longer any old predetermined emotional binaries to be followed. A new binary has now been created to re-start a new story.

The old exercise is finished. What now? When our research discovered this path, I was overjoyed.

Previous material had informed us that the indigo children or new souls in the eighties were new souls. They informed us that they were brand new and we automatically presumed, they were like new born babies, but we only knew half the facts.

It would take me another twenty year to discover the truth through hypnotherapy. It was far more exciting than the death of one soul and the birth of a new one. That synopsis created the death of immortality and influenced the ideologies of an eternal hell.

Our new research prolonged the continuum of immortality however with a bonus gift of ongoing new life as well. What this does is eliminate all fear of death completely for everyone.

Within each one of your timelines, as in a suicide for example, from your initial discerned judgement of emotional injustice, to the final endgame, you may have to experience five maybe six lifetimes. With each existence your binary transforms you physically more and more into the image of the suicide victim.

Due to the synchronicity of the timeline with each existence, at the same time at the same age, with the same impact, you will emotionally ask again and transform more, so as to alter more of your binaries so you will become the exact embodiment of that original victim.

This your predetermined gaseous path and you will take it to the end. You designed this tormenting emotional injustice through a simple question. Now, you too experience all of it so you will eventually understand unimaginable love and self-empowerment.

This timeline continues at exactly the same time with the same impact through every existence until you are the exact replica of your original victim physically and emotionally. Once you are completely one with the suicide victim your story is complete, it is over.

It is like designing a car. You draw the design and each week you add more and more to the manufacturing of your car until your car and the original design are alike and it leaves the car room. Finished.

Now like the Lego man an amazing transformation takes place. You are reborn as a new being, without any past life recriminations binding you. You have to start again. Thus, embryos use the path of miscarriage or abortion to obtain new DNA only, to begin or return to their new journey.

While researching this path we also opened unusual doors to different paths. Other paths that were also deemed as mortal sins however, they could also be deemed as man-made hell. For if the suicide victim was free from supposed hell and we all are immortal, then so are the evil ones. What happened to those doomed beings?

This path was even more exciting and demonstrated how victimised we become through fear mongering religions and old dogmas. It also clarified how all the old teachings could only be divulged from the individual perspective of the teacher.

They were actually incapable of understanding the true magnificence of the cosmic principles, and when the truths were presented to them, they were declined due to their inability to grasp such a magnitude of intelligence.

They still believed the world was flat and the centre of the entire universe between two planes up until the 16th century. They didn't or couldn't fathom that the earth was round.

You would seriously think that if you were connected to an almighty Divine force it would have revealed to you that vital piece of information.

These religious fear mongering teachers were still murdering innocence who revealed the truth in the 17th century. Yet, in today's society many are still forced to believe the spiritual dogma of that time as testament from a muscle toned titanic Godhead sitting up there somewhere.

To express that earth in comparison to the rest of the universe is nothing but invisible space dust, made up of zillions of invisible cells and really doesn't exist as we see it, would have been mystifying shamanic heresy. "Off with their heads!"

The smallness and littleness of their intelligence is expressed in their ego-maniacal dogmas, so to try to explain our immortality would have been sacrilege.

Once an endgame is completed and there are no more tasks to perform; the victim's the slate is clean. In essence, the being becomes a new energy. It has basic data with no future program. All information regarding their past life perceptions have been erased.

In our original assessments this new infant was still drawn forward by a higher consciousness but it had no individual information, no direction. However, with the Slav gypsy information and the belated relationship information, new evaluations have been calculated and included to testify to the reason and the path behind our new binary theory.

This infant bonds with a family member they were previously existing with and redeems their old DNA lineage only. It then moves on quickly by having the miscarriage or abortion, so it can return later as a grand- child or great grandchild. IVF is the same. The infant redeems the parent's DNA either mother or father.

If this is the first child, the DNA redeemed is from one of the parent's information only. If there are other older siblings, the infant retrieves all the DNA from the parents and all older siblings chronologically. The last sibling will become either the parent or grandparent of this new being.

> *"It is in the judging you shall be judged, to the full extent of your measuring stick."*

Matrix wise, by emotionally querying some impact about a said crime, you re-program your binary to personify the same emotional format for you to experience same said crime. You just wrote your script to your future timeline.

In every existence at the same time and with the same impact you will re-live that scenario again. If you question again it will replay again and again and again until the crime has been committed by you.

But, what if you don't? I don't just mean sweep it under the mat; no; I mean what if you determinedly decide to alter your attitude completely?

How do you stop it from involving you and evolving you?

1. When a disturbing occurrence appears before you, first you recognise that the person or obstruction in front of you is in victim mode. They or it is in front of you informing you of a past life occurrence that took place at the same time, same age and same impact. They are displaying your past life and your future life behaviour as one. If you question again you too will remain in victim mode and continue.
2. Realise that this karmic timeline is informing you that this path has already been completed and repeated by you and them several times before and today it is re-occurring again.
3. Karmic wise everything is as it should be. You are being informed that if you react again you will walk the same path of the obstruction again only in opposite to equal value. You will be the perpetrator instead of victim.

This point of realisation should free you from any future paths of injustice. By realising that you have already taken this path from many different emotional formats of emotion before, you can now choose to walk free.

Judgement has nothing to do with so called final judgment which doesn't exist. In the old thesis of life, everything had beginnings and endings, they couldn't comprehend nothing-ness, endlessness or immortality; that pleasure was only for omnipotent Gods.

It is in *your* everyday questions from superior or inferior judgements of your life around you that you will uncover your vicitmising injustices for you to experience in either this life or the next. The words, the actions, the reaction of others are all informing you of your status.

With each discerned judgement or opinion, you instantly alter your binary codes in each and every cell throughout your body and beyond; they then start embodying you physically as that emotion; it grows, upgrades, expands alters your chromosomes with each and every lifetime.

You transfigure into the new rendition of the murderer and continue your new journey as the murderer. But the embodiment of a murderer is only represented by a specific accumulation of various emotional binary codes. To experience that depth of irrational torturous injustice you can only travel the path of that type of murder, from wars to genocide to accidental manslaughter. That binary code depicts that specific outcome only.

Judgement is the instinctive ego of superiority. Within of your psyche is an extract of the binary code of this narcissistic emotion that compels you to feel so superior to other's that lives are meaningless.

In your next life you will be forced to experience the extremity of that narcissistic emotion from the opposite perspective. Your binary codes will match murderers and abusers. This is the equal value of your instinctive judgement.

These feelings of emotional injustices are what you have to reconcile within you. The cold emotionless supercilious invincible narcissist with your wretched worthless powerless vicitmised self. By recognising you have walked both paths consistently for 200000 years and you experienced all sides of it to their fullest, you realise this path is finished. You don't have to walk it any more. Now you are deliberately choosing not to be controlled by this path anymore. You are now experiencing FREEDOM. You are now experiencing real JUSTICE

These are two extremes of one emotion; By uniting them equally as one you are accepting that you cannot have one without the other. Once you have achieved the knowledge that neither are superior nor inferior you can allow them to exist without you.

Now allow yourself to be empowered

Like the murderer and paedophile, the people left behind judging, will follow suit because they are imprisoned in their own emotional timeline of injustice. This ongoing never-ending timeline is inevitable; but it no longer has to be for you.

Bear in mind, it is not the act of suicide or murder that is the issue; it is simply the lethal ramifications of that path of that particular emotion. The answer to your question. It is the emotional judgements, or someone's personal interpretation of that emotional injustice that had to be experienced. Knowing that you now understand that path and that it led to your freedom, you no longer need ask.

What the family left behind have to now realise is the path is simply a path. It is their vicitmising pain that incarcerates them and will continue to imprison them for as long as they ask, or until they no longer wish to experience their victimisation. This is not personal.

When we can allow death, the reincarnational continuum and the theories that timelines do force history to repeat itself as a part of life;

When you can live and know that you will see departed children again in your possible life time;

Will that assist you in stopping you from asking about the unrelenting emotional injustice and victimisation of losing a child, that you really do not have to endure?

Will educating women with the truth and exposing them to facts that challenge past life beliefs, at the same time eliminating the predisposed horrors of those teaching's, principles; will that forge us finally ahead to out find our true paths of Freedom.

Will uncovering the truths that were quashed due to authoritarian financial greed, assist us to overturn our fanatical old beliefs and open doors to future paths that now reveal, with proof, that life, death and resurrection are an ongoing process of our immortality.

Will realising that the key to your future happiness lies in your understanding that you already have everything you could possibly desire and more and in knowing that you don't have to ask,

You simply have to learn to allow,
Would you take that key?

I AM FREEDOM

NOW CAN YOU SEE ME?

Chapter Fourteen

THE DIABOLICAL PATH

I AM HELL

To understand how past life hypnotherapy regressions works you have to find someone who has experienced the episode or as they say, has a guide who is able to divulge the information to you, knowing the ongoing purpose of that information.

With the assistance of Big John and Little John again, the one path I found difficult to research was the one in reference to Germany in WW2 where many of the accused chemical and murdering assailants who performed horrendous acts of atrocity, committed suicide when they were convicted of their crimes and sentenced to a firing squad.

This suicide was not like other suicides, it was not out of mental pain or anguish. In fact, there was no pain. This again to me (my perception) was egocentric narcissistic power playing.

Our suicide research discovered, up to this stage, the participant of the suicide returned within a short period, not necessarily to the same lineage, country or to the same family, but with a good intent to begin a new life again.

However, there is another form of suicide and these are the ones who not only condemn the act of suicide but an ongoing form of mortal hell as well, they then ensue this path according to their justification.

The emotional injustice incurred is specific to their voiced opinion. This specific pain they physically and emotionally experience is strictly information divulging the answer to their condemnation and their voiced judgment.

Once the suicide has taken place instead of it being the end of their path, they continue on the next part of their journey to experience their further injustice voiced by their opinion. This specific experience of emotional injustice again has only one explicit path. It will reveal to them every emotional injustice comprised from all levels for them to experience their answer to their interpretation of hell.

This narcissistic form of suicide was where we uncovered this new continuum. Another agonising type of timeline, that is pursued with the act of suicide.

This ongoing timeline continued a journey through karmic retribution. Opposite effect of equal value of the same historical scenarios over and over again in a timeline loop. However, this is the timeline of ongoing persecution and immense suffering, as opposed to new life.

The period between existences was still short and specific. In other words, instead of waiting a century to return to experience their next life as we normally do, the consequences of all suicide victims are the urgency to finish uncompleted business. They return swiftly within ten to twenty-year period to recommence the next part of their journey in a new binary matched body, who is on the same journey.

Both paths are karmic and are dependent on the voiced emotional judgements before the original suicide.

From their perspectives, their focus is more on the doomed path of hell, rather than on the act of suicide.

Mid twentieth century the WWII mastermind criminals were empowering their pride of the superior warrior, their victory. These German wartime veterans saw themselves as supreme beings and others as minor races, rats, animals to be used and abused.

Slavs and many other European races were accused as being unworthy. The Germans assumed they had the right to use other humans as animals, "test guinea pigs." Hitler encouraged them to believe themselves to be the descendants of an Aaryn race, pure supreme and not of a bohemically mixed race.

This actions not only echoed the crusades of the past; these actions procured by these dehumanising dictators replicated the exact same demoralising opinions of the latter Americans as in their comments, re; The Marshall Islanders; *"they are not like us; we are civilised; but they resemble us more closely than mice."*

The German nation refused to take responsibility for their ignorance and stated that, their experimental actions, *"were for the benefit and advancement of human kind."* This barbaric verbalisation was also echoed throughout past history and was strongly reiterated through the latter American injudiciousness.

Our hypnotherapy research revealed that all suicides return early due to unfinish business; it also iterated how, *word for word,* it is through this verbal lie, in the timeline that history repeats itself exactly.

I deduced from this evidence that there was a possibility that within an extremely short period, these suicide fatalities may have become victims of their own horror stories, to the very same narcissistic supremacism that they bestowed within the same century?

If this is so, it doesn't justify these actions, it only reinforces the theories of how our timelines keep repeating themselves, until we realise, we are creating them and need to rectify them.

None of these practices should ever have been allowed to be carried out, however, in all cases the countries of the offenders embraced and empowered their superior's arrogance and sat back and denied any knowledge of any bad conduct or genocide. All countries dating back to 324AD, had the same verbal designs; on becoming the next super power or leader of the world.

If hell exists, then for me, all of these atrocities reveal a possible path. The algorithmic equation of the timeline of history repeating itself, revealed many of the original bio chemists of WWII should become their own victims in that century twenty years later. Once that has occurred, they will then match the normal karmic timeline loop of this ongoing hell and continue experiencing it for centuries until they stop it.

Many of the suicidal bio-chemists of WWII, who test dummied the innocent men, women and children in WWII, would have instantly physically transformed into their victims with every act of cruelty, preparing them swiftly for the next part of their karmic journey as victims.

AT the end of the WWII 1945-1991 bio chemists occupied the Marshall Islands, then with 67 nuclear bombs and missiles proceeded to use the island as a chemical testing ground and the inhabitants as *chemical test guinea pigs*.

The Vietnam war from 1961-1991 Dioxin from Agent Orange, sprayed by the US military during the Vietnam war, is still poisoning Vietnamese people today, 30-40 years after spraying ended.

Suicide victims recalibrate their binary codes swiftly to continue their rapid journey in a close-range timeline. These biochemist/suicide victims were programmed to become victims of chemical warfare immediately by other bio chemists. Once that action was procured, they now continue their normal karmic journey of cause and effect until it is done.

The future paths for all the bio chemists and victims are now in a timeline loop of ongoing chemical warfare over and over again until they stop it.

The short timeline match; the verbal voicings match; and the final impacts match. Karmic retribution state opposite and equal value. This path echoes a very strong possibility. To me this would-be hell.

We have had to always to rely on scribes to tell the tales, but today in this computer age, the ongoing repeated histories of all last centuries onslaughts were visually experienced by everyone in the world through telecommunication in their own home every night.

All these ongoing repeated loops of war were exposed before all of us in a very short time period. We have experienced this century after century as well. We have been here before and if we remain in victim mode, we will experience it all again. These inevitable paths have already been determined.

Is there a possibility or probability of it all happening again this century? Due to the proven historical timeline theory, it is very real. When you mathematically do the deductions based on thousands of years of invasions in our past life time histories dating back to Alexander the great and further, these possibilities are extremely high.

When a probability timeline flashes up in front of you as it has; the possibilities are like the gaseous flare predictions for the fires. This may be the first time in history we are able to forecast a probable world atrocity.

When you can see an objectionable future timeline approaching you, due to the rules of history repeating itself, and you have the opportunity to alter it to a better one; why wouldn't you want to try?

Regardless of the fact that these paths may be answers to a possible hell, we have seen it now. We know what it looks like, how it works, and how it ends. Do we really have to remain victim to this experience again?

Or as usual will we sit back in disbelief and allow the narcissistic civilised educated men to step up, as they do, and dictate the rules again, and as they do in situations of war; create a new ongoing war timeline mid this century. Was my friend in the elevator physically informing me? This is the future path determined for all of us?

Future generations have to be open to new and ongoing continuum theories instead of impractical dogma that utterly refuses to investigate other possible options. The old suppositions leave too many people victimised in drastic traumatic experiences empowering emotional injustices to continue karmic timelines we no longer need to experience.

The teachings of yore no longer have the real answers needed to continue through the new millennium.

The next generation are more advanced contemporaries, and the old fight to survive orientated dogmas of the past simply do not function any more.

Every day we are re-living our past life loops in a world that is walking, talking, visible proof of all our past life practices. Continuous victimisation formed from unceasing emotional injustices. Victimisation, be it from a pope a bishop a priest, a king, a queen, a leader, a politician, a boss, a manger, a department head, a bank, a school, a hospital, an aged care facility, or a nursing home and carer, is still powerlessness and persecuted emotional abuse.

The world is not doing it to us; it is exposing us to us.

When you recognise the victim in them, you should also see the victim in you. When you understand how they have vicitmised everyone in the past, you also should understand how you victimised everyone in your past. You are re-living your entire story, through the mirror, in your now.

We are all victims of Adam's need to survive. It's a state of mind. As victims our Eve binary code is shuddering in fear of Adam's might. We are obedient, insignificant, uneducated, and his slave. He is civilised and educated. We as his victimised EVE are his enablers.

I as Eve empowered my ongoing maze of instinctual fears for years. I wore my garments for over sixty years this time and I didn't know I was wearing them. I was re-living all my timeline loops of obedient victimisation over and over again. I unknowingly imprisoned me in my incessant world of material justice.

Through this life I kept repeating the same indignations over and over again. I kept creating my own prison. It didn't hold me, I did. I was always free to leave at any time, but I kept empowering any and every emotion of injustice that exposed itself to me and inadvertently CHOSE to stay.

To be born so frozen as I was; the timeline I was re-living re-exposed those same ideologies with those same puritan moralities, imprisoning me yet again to a world of humongous guilt, fear, powerlessness, self-hatred and undying obedience without question.

Every person expressed it to me; performed it in front of me. In one form or another, I have borne this suit of victimised obedience for the full 20000 centuries at least as a woman, since the beginning of time.

All my studies and interests this life time constantly revealed the oppressive behaviour of all the egocentric leaders of the past over their victimised communities. This was also revealing my lifelong timelines. For centuries they were cold, heartless and frozen; so was I.

The split in the dynamics and the fallacy that was then empowered, was the principle that we live in a duality existence. We do; however, the fallacy infers that this is how it has to be.

If as an inferior being you challenged this principle you were slain, drowned, raped, murdered, massacred through genocide, burned to the stake, your property stolen, your reputation slandered, you were enslaved to abhorrent brutality and your family imprisoned and starved. As Buddha says;

"The lesson will continue until it is learnt."

The lesson if not learnt will always evolve get bigger. It will continue in an ongoing loop. It upgrades, develops, enlarges, evolves like everything else however, the original emotion of the injustice or story is and will remain the original force.

The victimising tools of fear; bigotry, racial discrimination, greed, insecurity is always used to manifest power and greed in the material world; this is Adam's dire need for dominance, supremacy, and survival. This is one of our never-ending timeline loops. This is our ongoing repetition; same time, same actions, same impact, same words, opposite genders, round and round.

All these emotional fear factors have produced our world as we see it today. Those original carnal needs to survive tactics that were created in our original timeline are still within us all. As our fears evolved, we evolved. It was through those carnal instincts that our now timelines continue to adapt.

From single celled amoeba to Nuclear warfare man the binaries have advanced. Instinct, survival, warrior, godhead; continually expanding, developing, and evolving.

Yet one dominant factor always remains; empowering one emotion over the other. The egocentric instinctual fear factor that *the strongest shall survive*.

As women now we can question authority without being knocked down. We can do whatever we want and no one can touch us. For the first time 200000 years, we are free.

Knowing that; when you are inundated by the intense pursuers of injustice, you now know that feeling of freedom; use it. All the evidence before you is telling you, this is who you were; this is what you did. You are
re-living it all again, in your now. This is how it ends.

Without witnessing all the evidence, you could never understand freedom, not without all the victimisation of all the intense imprisonments. Every insignificant component played an important part in your emancipation and is vital information for your independence

Does hell exist? When you are on the receiving end of the atrocities of war, yes not only does it exist it will continue for the victims until they realise, they are feeding it. With every act of indecency, the victim will react, question and engage in transforming their binary codes to become the infiltrator of those injustices.

The more intense the barbarism, the more intense the focus. Unfortunately, yes, the victim will become the perpetrator and carry out the very same acts they are voicing. For it is in their voicing that they write their script.

When this person is in front of you voicing their articulate opinion; know that you too have followed both of these paths. Open your mind and understand that you are able to see the future outcomes for both of you.

This is not the only time both of you have experienced this. You are caught up in this phenomenally barbaric karmic war loop. You are both re-living it again from the opposite perspectives and it will continue until you both choose to no longer walk it.

By questioning and reacting you are recreating your future path to the exact words of your story. After 700000 battles ranging from arrows to nuclear bombs, you are now allowed to realise that you have experience all that hell has to offer. You know what it looks like, feels like, and how it ends.

You now have the option to make a new choice.
Remain a victim to the injustices of war or FREEDOM
You have the key.

Now you understand how freedom feels, you have the choice. You can continue to walk the ongoing loop of vicitmised hell or you can choose

FREEDOM

I WAS HELL

NOW CAN YOU SEE ME?

Chapter Fifteen

I WAS SPLENDID

NOW SEE ME

We can't alter the past timelines; we can't alter the present timelines; but we can realise them and alter our futures outcomes. There are 7 billon people in the world today and every one of them mirror your nano emotions within you at this very moment. Like the Milky Way they are exactly the same as you, just emotionally ratioed differently.

To clarify: you may be constructed of 60% love and 40% anger: your neighbour may be 20% anger 20% rage and 40% love. We are all made up of emotions but our ratios are different.

We all have experienced every one of them through our paths of injustice at one time or another thus creating a new evolved emotion.

Today there are 7 billion various ratios of emotions mirroring you in one form or another but they are created and moulded from the same molecular structure as you.

Our world is the evolutionary product of Adam's warrior world only now we exist in a nuclear environment. That initial instinctual judgement defined by him as being more superior, godlike, and stronger than any other being in his existence, still defines all of us in our fighter mode today, only now it is nuclear.

Our leaders and teachers of today still enforce these old instinctive doctrines. Don't give up; Don't be a coward; Fight back. But these superior positions enforce the fight. Then as obedient enablers we empower another fight; their fight.

What they don't realise is that they are teaching you to re-create a fight within us all. They are conditioning you to believe that the weaker or lessor side of you is not good enough. You have to be the strong warrior, the bully, the narcissist who fights all odds without contention. However, that principle designs you to walk a path of your victim in your next life.

There are more of us than there are leaders. We are the ones who put them there. We allow them to govern our future path. Learn to choose leaders who equalise our future paths.

How many times have you gone to the polls and felt that the one you have to vote for is "the best of a bad bunch?"

Of course, you have, for they are all supported by the same capitalistic financial institutions that dictate which country is allowed to be financially successful this season and which innocent country, for a huge profit, will fall.

This reaction is classed as "conspiracy theories." The truth is, there wouldn't be conspiracy theories if our leaders and establishment could be trusted. So, if you cannot trust the hierarchy, then who can you trust?

I could say "you," but at this stage, is that the truth?

To get to the stage where you can trust you completely, you have to redesign yourself to become someone you can trust completely. Someone who understands that your future happiness is within your grasp, you simply have to allow. This is the next path of your new Lego duplication.

You have to know ***your*** ethics, morals and values and be proud to wear them as your garment. You have to be able recognise when and how your ego is questioning.

With this new attitude, to do that you have to find out who you really want to be and design yourself to transform into that person. Most of my work is predisposed to women. That is because for the first time in history ever, we are learning to be women in women's' bodies, as a woman. As a woman I am now allowed to teach as a woman.

Our group consisted of some amazing men, and I respected and loved them as work colleagues, but they are no longer with me, and I believe there is a reason for that. Our work was collaborated, but when the dissertations were dispensed, I was teaching them from the male perspective. I was a female dressed in male clothing. I now carry on the work, but from a real woman's perspective now.

I am no longer a female version of Adam and I am not a female version of his enabler Eve either. The men of the world are happy where they are and that is fine. However, for centuries, the world has and is still displaying all that you are capable of delivering.

I've lived it, I know how it works and I 've seen how it ends.

Women also think as mothers. So, by freeing them, they can teach and free future nations in each existence as either male or female.

First and foremost; it's not that this path was ever taken from us; it is that we have never been offered this before. We are becoming empowered *women* for the first time in existence as well as educated women in our own right. However, our education is not the same dogma as our past. It not only empowers women, it empowers everyone, without raising a finger.

Two, we are female, meaning feminine. Meaning we are not men dressed up in women's clothing. We are no longer the front man for their capitalistic dogma. Simply by standing up beside the men does not empower us. The male capitalistic rules still applied, only now women have to enforce them in a dress.

Three you are a voluptuous woman. Don't care how you look; know you are more. Shine from the inside, believe me, people do notice.

Four, as a real woman you can make a huge difference to you, your family and your world simply by being you. You now have to think like the real woman you want to be. There're no rules; well, there is one.

You are no longer victim to the carnal beliefs of xenophobic obedience. You are no longer the victimised enabler of any carnal narcissist, male or female.

It doesn't matter what you look like, it is who you want to become. You created this magnificent woman from Nirvana; now be that woman. If you appreciate what you see and smell like, you at least can smile at yourself; this is where we will start.

We filled your entire inner silhouette from the inside out with inner assurance, and without raising a finger, the response was amazing. Now, we address from the outside to the inside. Let's dress us up a little.

My wardrobe had clothes that dated back to the sixties. When we did the declutter, I simply tossed many of the clothes that annoyed me. That left me with a basic wardrobe.

What my daughter then asked was a brilliant question I had never asked myself. What are your colours? How do you want to present yourself?

If you have to redesign you, what colours are you going to wear? Many of us buy what we see on sale or in a shop because it speaks to you in some way about your mood at that moment.

Now you are a determined presence. What colours would present you to your new world. What colours do you want your bedroom to be? What colours do you want to surround you? What colours say to you "THIS IS ME; WOMAN."

This does not mean you will be some major force to be beckoned with, this means as a real free woman who is no longer a victim of any circumstances. You are allowed to stand tall now; smile and shine from the inside out.

Now you can say; this is me on a sunny day; this is me on a cool day; this is me on an autumn day or winter day or shopping day or coffee day. Refrain from overcrowding, keep it simple and svelte. I like that word; it means classic and graceful.

I found a combination of five colours that defined me as a person and I felt very comfortable in them.

I did the same for my bedroom. I created my ambience and it created an inner sanctuary of luxury. This simple exercise gave me grounding in who I wish to portray as me.

The next redefining chapter was with my perfumes or how I smelt. What fragrance did I want to permeate my surroundings both to my outside world and me? Over the years I have had my signature perfume but when I started taking care of my mother, I let it slide. Then when

I returned to purchase them again, they were either deleted or I didn't appreciate them anymore.

It took a while, but I found four and they all have my new romantic feminine *signature*. The first one is for my shower. Due to my low lung capacity, I have difficulty getting oxygen to my skin and it dehydrates easily, so a soft sensitive perfumed cream after my shower is an important regime for me. My shower perfume is complimentary to the cream. It's refreshing and makes me feel sensual, soft and invigorated. It lingers in the bathroom and acts as a romantic room deodorant as well.

For those who are married; this is the one where hubby comes up and cuddles you from behind and kisses you on the neck and says "wow you smell nice."

My bed perfume has to snuggle. This is sprayed on my bed linen, nighties, pyjamas and bed underwear. My mum used to use talcum powder and her bed always smelt divine. To sit on her bed to chat or even enter her bedroom was heavenly. Now I have that same sensual ambiance.

Next is my shopping or work perfume. This is for my daily shopping, clothes and me. It has to be comfortable, feminine but not over-whelming. It has to be one where people walk past you and react with, "mm that's nice" why?

Because the new you is no longer invisible. Be prepared for that. Strangers both male and female do come out of the woodworks and chat. What they say to you is important for *the words voiced* are feedback on your progress.

Your scent has to give you the confidence you need in knowing people will either look or comment. You have to be able to walk with your head held high, knowing that the new you, is the you, that you want to express to your new world. Your binary is upgrading, so your environment is upgrading as well.

Your scents have to present the you, that you wish to represent.

So many women walk through shopping centres with their head looking at the floor. The older they grow the worse they become. No more. You are no longer invisible to anyone. You no longer hide your beautiful face from anyone.

STOP HIDING IN YOUR PAST.

Remember this is for you, as your new empowered Eve. Someone we have never seen or been before, ever. Now your outside world will automatically match you. Knowing that you are not only making a difference within you but your outer world as well, should boost that inner confidence of beauty and equality.

You are not standing up and fighting or protesting; You are empowering all of you from the inside, which is empowering all of them at the same time with the same impact. You are all quietly creating new binary codes within you which is immediately transforming all of you to new amazing men and woman with new future paths amazing timeline. Each and every one of the people in your environment will now have a wondrous experience in their next existence and no one knows you're doing it.

Finally, your investment perfume; only one. Take your time with this one. Single or married, this must be the one that seduces, teases, taunts, and sexually inspires you and your partner if you have one. This is the one that stays all over you, him and the linen, all night long. This is the one that takes you from house wife, mother, grandmother, mother-in-law, worker, caretaker, gardener, kitchen hand to sex goddess.

This is the one that takes you from the peck on the cheek "goodnight hon," to "lock the doors darling, this is gonna be an all-nighter with breakfast in bed."

This baby goes all over you from top to bottom. There is only one important fact. If you are married, your partner must like it also. This is your "oh yeah!" perfume.

So now you have your inner confidence, your wardrobe, your style, and your perfumes to compliment the womanly female component of your Eve you want to be. This outer insurance compliments and strengthens your inner assurance.

The perfumes are your artistic expression of how you need to feel inside about yourself. By saying, I am Eve, I am proud to be woman, is having the courage to allow the centuries of carnal abuse we have endured through false beliefs for centuries to exist without your participation. We are forced to continually re-live these fallacies today. They may not be as obvious, but they do still exist. However, we no longer have to entertain them.

By saying to yourself, I am beautiful by just being me and I am not some marketing material sex object; I am no longer a slave or victim to male competitiveness or commercialisation. The clothes and perfumes I buy have a specific purpose. They are part of my inevitable future I gave to me. They are not simply marketing trash. They express the future prosperous me; for I am not lessor nor superior to anyone. I am equal to all that I am, as I am.

The things you buy for yourself in this way are score cards informing you of your personal inner value. Your outside world will evaluate your success. You've now established an ethical and moral ground to stand on and be proud of. Your inner self power will exude to your outer world. You have united your worlds.

These simple alterations redefine your binary codes and your DNA with every new thought word and physical modification. You're allowing your future success to come to you to formulate your next timeline along with all those you have impacted. They will also be people of self-assurance, self-confidence, equality, self-empowerment, and non-victimisation.

These amazing binaries will radiate through your unseen cells, beyond your body, your environment, your limitations, beyond your beliefs, beyond your world.

That is important for personal self-empowerment. You are doing this all for YOU no one else. But the more you do it, the more the outside world reciprocates. You are not altering the world; your binaries are matching them with like-minded binaries and together you all are all altering the world, peacefully.

However, the more confident you become, the more you meet these types of encouraging people. The more you all encourage each other, the more everyone's self-empowerment glows, and grows. A consciousness of a heaven can exist also.

Now add this new self-confident outer voluptuousness of womanhood to your Lego. Allow others to do the same to theirs both male and female in their own time.

CAREER PATH OR CREATIVE PATH

Mid-sixties Pat Robertson stated, "never allow women to be liberated for they will destroy capitalism." He was voicing his low opinion on the stupidity of womanhood, and the practicalities of allowing them in positions of prominence.

Regardless of how you feel inside, if your outside world reflects carnal anguish or lack then you are receiving feedback of an emotional injustice taking place within you. If your job or career is patronising, demeaning or even non interesting, this is a department of self-slavery and low self-esteem. If you are working for the money, you are caught up in the male world of capitalism. You are re-living your emotional injustice timeline of past victimised poverty.

As this new vibrant woman, you are being informed, you've done this in your past. Not this job necessarily but this debasing slavery. You've experienced it, you've seen it, you know how it works and you know how it ends. If you are being shown this, it has a purpose. Due to your new attitude of *allowance,* your inevitable future path of amazing prosperity and abundance is displaying what fortune is not. Now you understand your own empowerment. You no longer ask; you no longer question; you allow.

When you are being given the option for change, the opportunity to make a different to your life; allow this new path to open up to you.

Instead of complaining about your job, know you are now being offered a much better option. Then allow all the doors to open. When you are this new person, resistance is futile, so learn to enjoy the ride.

Your amazing prosperous path already exists, now regardless of how stupid it sounds, allow it to all come to you. As Walt Disney said, "the crazier it was, the more successful I knew it would be."

We, as women in the work force have followed in men's footsteps since we were allowed to start. They were always materialistic, competitive and capitalistic. This was all the knew. This is all they can offer you.

Your life, your career is meant to be exciting, fulfilling, enriching and exhilarating as well as prosperous and opulent.

It has always been about the gold for men dating back centuries. Just because men work this way, does not mean it is the most successful way to work, and this is the key to Eve's future success.

If you remain working in the same way men work, you will not progress any further than they have and what's more, you will have to answer to them forever. This is another path of your past victimisation exposing itself.

Einstein said; *"you cannot remedy a problem using the same tools that created the problem."*

Marilyn Monroe said; *"any woman who want to be equal to a man, lacks ambition."*

There is another choice a better choice. In today's society, because you have not been informed of a better way, you are following their practices. You are working for the money and that will not bring you the happiness or self-empowerment you truly desire. Money is no more than the score card. It's how you earn the material advantages that brings the happiness, the rewards.

Like your new empowered education; it's not that you can't do it; It is one, that no one ever offered it to you, and two it doesn't exist yet.

Research the most successful entrepreneurs you have heard of and learn from them.

Bill Gate's dream was for everyone equally to have a computer in their home. No sooner had he upgraded and marketed one computer system, when he was regenerating a next one, even better, faster, more apps, for everyone to enjoy. The material rewards took care of themselves indicating the size of his success. He enjoyed creating and upgrading and developing. That is what his dreams was about. That vision is what he took with him when he passed away.

He didn't have to answer to governmental, dictatorial, bombastic bad behaviour. He was an entrepreneur. He paid his taxes; he maintained legal procedures; but he was his own man; he always will be in every life time. His binary upgraded and he had to leave us. His dream is the emotional timeline he created for him to continually experience.

He didn't empower the money or materialistic things of life; he empowered his dreams from every direction and with every ounce of emotional enthusiasm he re-empowered his DNA transforming physically into a new more empowering person in his next life. He refused to empower any injustice within him. He energised all his creative emotions equality. He allowed his dreams to express themselves through him with mindboggling results.

Walt Disney, Colonel Sanders are others who did the same. They didn't follow the morals of divided capitalism. They expressed the power of all their passionate dreams and exploded with creativity; as a result, they received enormous annuity in response. Abundance and prosperity beyond their wildest imaginations; but still only the score card.

This is your gift to you. Inside of you now is your magical inspirational dream; your vision from your future path, for you to create and be your own master now. It is the one thing no one else can touch or take from you. That wondrous dream you desire more than life itself; the dream of dreams. You created it; it already exists now; allow it to come to you; allow it to empower you; allow it to express itself through you.

It may be instead of making chocolate caramel slices with tonnes of sugar, you can create it with dates cacao and tahini. Consign it to a corner coffee shop, who wants to sell locally made healthy food. Because your future success is already predetermined find your inner creative entrepreneur and let your wildest dreams find your outlets.

When you are unsure of your dream, cling to your feeling inside of already achieving it. Then when an inspiration starts bugging you, have the courage to step out and follow it. Things around you start to generate activity. Everything starts happening faster. You learn to think on your spinning feet.

Before you start any of this, you have to check if your old job still has you bound in some victimised relationship with poverty. This is your old ego. You have to re-check your relationship with wealth. Ensure you are not empowering materialism over happiness. Materialism provides materialism only. True inspirations provide everything.

Refrain from allowing your old carnal fear factor to dictate your lifestyle. Allow your creativity to flourish. Don't run away from it; You will always wonder what would have happened? **Walk into it smiling** with your head held high and confidence raging. You won't be a billionaire in two weeks, but you will feel like a billionaire in two weeks.

Make sure you love what you want to do. It has to be something so special, that when you get up in the morning you cannot wait to get started. At three o clock in the morning, you are creating better ideas. You're not tired; you are excited. And if you had the choice you would do this even if you weren't paid; but you truly will be paid.

You can do anything you want. You can be anyone you want. You can go anywhere you want. There is nothing stopping you now.

You may reply, but I have the kids, the husband, the school, charity club, the football club, that's fine. But is that the future you want for them? If it is then you are on the right path. But if it's not, recognise your inner potential, your inner freedom. Your future path has also allowed for them, so you too allow them to be part of your equation and don't be afraid to fly; really high.

Now the practical side. One of the biggest drawbacks of independent business owners or entrepreneurs is when they start worrying about the expenses and the money. Your egocentric fear then determines your future path. Material gains are strictly feedback on how big your dream's is. Once you have created and made your third batch of cakes you may now be able to buy that fridge. The fridge is not the reason you are creating the cakes, it is simply informing you of the ratio and speed of your success.

It's not wrong to want material things; they simply aren't allowed to be the reason you live.

Hire an accountant; reason being; they take your mind off the petty things. If you start worrying about the money side of things, then you empower the money and the fear of the money starts determining the outcome of your dream. You go broke. That's why many businesses fail and why all the greats have a business partner.

Bill Gates, Walt Disney, Colonel Sanders, they enjoyed creating, while the business minded geniuses incessantly worried about how they would get the money. Walt Disney was quoted as saying, "that he would run an idea past his business partners or devil's advocates and if they didn't like it, he would go ahead with it, for it was certain to be a success. The stranger and more unique the idea, the more chance of its unrestricted unique success."

When you have that "GUT" feeling, it is the inner passion exploding within you. It has a need, a drive, an urgency, and if you do not follow, it will combust and go elsewhere.

This is *your* dream, follow it. Don't give it away to someone else because you are re-living some old emotional injustice that is rearing its ugly head again. If you do, that fear, that lack of courage will determine not only this path but your future paths as well and someone else, who had the same binary as you will get to experience the success of your dream. Fear always makes you fail.

It is scary; it is frightening; it's also exciting, but these divided emotions are destroying your future chances of success. Understand the power and strength of your fear. Know that without it you would not understand your bravery.

Now allow the power of the pleasure of your creativity to forge you ahead. Know that every nano second, every thought word and action is altering your DNA and chromosomes to physically create an embodiment of unbelievable success for you to wear.

The annoyance is the scratch. It's an itch. They niggle; your ego is testing your senses. These are good, for it is as if they are checking to see if you are listening. These usually have a materialistic value attached to them.

Get rich schemes, pyramid schemes, they have potential, and you will learn a lot but, in many cases, you are re-living some question of your past. You will lose your money for you are usually coming from a consciousness of need or lack, want to get rich quick.

This could mean you were scammed in a past life and reacted badly and have to relearn the lesson or worse; you scammed others out of their possessions and the table now has been turned. Either way, don't beat yourself up. Acknowledge that this timeline has been rectified, and when you progress forward this time it will be with the right intentions of equality for all, not just for the money. No forgiveness or guilt is necessary. That path was everybody's choice due to the same question being asked. Now everybody knows the answer.

Lets' evaluate our progress We realise we are an amazing new breed of women and we compliment that with our colour schemes, styles and perfumes. We now allow the success of our future paths to come to us, as opposed to searching for it.

We energise our inner feelings of self-empowerment and self-love to their highest potential to maintain focus. This attracts likeminded people, places and careers to us. This keeps us alive and motivated and in our high-flying motion.

By exuding this new woman from inside of you it will now explode in your outside world as well, "That's your real equality, that's your true self-empowerment." That's the new independent career woman or man we now add to our Lego.

To vanquish all the denigrations of the past we have to erase the shame of our sexuality. We have to allow ourselves to also be sexually attractive without guilt. We respond to Montaigne comment of, "sex with a woman is not like shitting in a bucket and tipping it on your head;

We cannot alter the insults of the past but, as the new breed self-empowered Eve, we are no longer victim to those forms of vituperations, and condemnations either.

WOW! With the new inner freedom, we are able to express today I can now create a sensually empowered woman who has the capability to make sex salacious, inviting, and erotic and not be condemned for feeling it. Having someone touching me is not an abomination of humors, vomit or bile. Martin Luther is also incorrect in enforcing his bible's teachings by saying I'm either wife or a whore. I am so much more.

A woman who enjoys sexual activity was classed as filthy, dirty, an unclean whore. The unclean component had to do with our menstrual cycle. This again only clarified their biological ignorance. The scribes were celibate, uneducated, pompous asses and civilised puritanic sexist bigots, they knew no better.

My world is no longer a world of duality as preached by old British/Hebrew/Judean/bibles. These sexual bigots were racist and created a world of double standards as preached by ignorant men. Women as obedient enablers have paid the price long enough for their indignant slurs.

This was another component of our Nirvana. Our future path is already overflowing with sexual enjoyment and happiness for you and your partner or partners. All we have to do now is allow it.

We now as the new breed of woman have already started displaying our inner sexuality. We are so resplendently voluptuous; we have the capability of being both a woman and a sexually attractive female with dignity and grace and the men who portray the same binaries as us will match it. We have the capability of showering them with sexual responsiveness and sensual adoration, and I can guarantee, unless they are still carnal, which means they are egocentric and their binaries do not match, they won't be complaining.

We as voluptuous females will no longer allow sexual victimisation from within us to divide us as women again due to some form of egocentric emotional injustice. We will embrace all our past emotional injustices and allow them all to exist but we do not have to play with them. Allow and wear the garment of all the empowerment of your inevitable fabulous future and create our new breed of sensual Eve and Adam united and evolved. That is the next block of our Lego.

Body of History

Women have the capability to stand alone in a world of capitalism, and regardless of what the old dictatorial dominating narcissists have said; that does not make us lesbians nor do we have something wrong with our sexual organs.

Now here is why we respond as opposed to react. The retribution in the timelines that lies ahead for all the despotic narcissists is of their own making. The more they deride the status quo of womanhood, the more they alter their DNA to experience their own derogatory remarks over and over again, either as woman or man, but not as equal.

It is in the noise making that we follow the paths of extremities. The noisy timelines of high and low waves. It is in our resistance that the DNA alters and they start replicating that very resistance.

This is the fluctuating wave of karmic resolution; the extremely high ups and downs.

We as women we must learn to remain quiet achievers and empower ourselves almost secretly from the inside. When you allow, there is a calmness within you, no egocentric reactions. Everything within you is neutralised and quiet, as one. Your future karmic resolution timeline is now flat and all is equal; we *value* all of it as one and it empowers all of us as one, without variables.

We cannot alter our past transgressions against us or by us to the world or others. We empowered our instinct over other emotions. That karmic timeline, continued on the same path of high up and downs in each of our lives over and over again until we balanced it. Now it is balanced.

That is why we learn to embrace the remarkable new breed women that we truly are, in silence. We have balanced our narcissist with our victim. We know we need both. That is why we allow our warrior to be the warrior, as opposed to reacting to him and fighting him. We need them both together for us to recognise our freedom and to detect any forms of egocentric injustice.

However, if another is directly in front of you, their attitude is exposing a past timeline for you to now rectify. You are re-living a past narcissistic carnal warrior verses your carnal victim again and they are exposing themselves again. This time you naturally recognised it. You know what to do; empower your allowing. Smile, because now, you've got this and you don't have to raise a finger.

No one taught us this in the past. The men didn't know it, they didn't understand it, they couldn't teach it, neither did the women. As a result, we all reacted and our history kept repeating itself over and over again.

Like the British who destroyed the oasis of Australia; like the Europeans who devoured the USA and like the Germans who vanquished Western Europe and England; the yanks who vaporised the Marshall Islands, or the nine nations that own the Amazon, they all knew what should have done, but materialism determined what they did. Now that emptiness will doom their futures not just once but over and over again until they understand.

They are like everyone else, they have been warned, over and over again, but the forewarnings fall on deaf supremist untouchable ears, now no one will hear their screams.

They saw it as occultism, mysticism, shamanic, in league with Satan. So, it isn't as if they weren't told. They deliberately chose these paths.

Simply because they are arrogant civilised bullies; simply because they have money; simply because they have a lot of tar and cement; doesn't make them champions, it simply makes them deaf, materialistic, empty headed, narcissists.

As the Cree stated.

"DO NOT CREATE A WORLD THAT YOU WILL NOT WANT TO RETURN TO, IN SEVEN GENERATIONS."

In other words, you will experience your unacceptable behaviour.

One more vital step. This is the last of the crucial paths that need to be clarified within you and placed in your Lego construction. Your creative source.

Your integral desires inside you from where you create now. You re-live you past in your now; all the feedback around you tells you what you did, how it worked, how you did it and how it ended. You are also living your future path now. It too is revealed in exactly the same way. However, there are two ways to determine your future path; one from your past path and two from your future.

By experiencing the senselessness of ongoing injustice in its billions of disguises, you now understand the magnificence of true inconceivable happiness. Let that feeling transform your binaries and match you with your future binaries now. That is what allowing is.

Out of the everything you receive nothing; that's your pastlife path.

Out of your nothingness, you will receive everything;
that's your all-embracing magnificent future

This is the last and the most vital component of your restructuring you as a breed of human. Whatever you define yourself as mentally will personify you, both now and in your future paths.

Liken to Mother Theresa, Gandhi, Mandela, know your values; allow them to define you for freedom for all equally and you will receive the same in gratis, karma does not judge, it only reacts to the same value.

By understanding this truth in reference to our
timelines and how we create them;

By understanding that the violent paths of immoral others are finished and concluded upon the victim's death and no longer concern you;

You should be able to release all your egocentric feelings of past life transgressors and refrain from empowering them incorrectly, thus, creating a new ongoing continuum based on your ego for you to follow.

This freedom of allowance has to make a difference to your values. No more stress for everything is taken care of; no more fear for your future is already reassured; what more could you want?

By understanding you are the most beautiful being in your existence and you created you just the way you are to expose your exquisiteness and the magnificence of the universe you exist in.

By understanding that you are no good to anyone else until you are amazing to yourself, so keep making yourself happy internally.

By understanding it's impossible to empower one emotion without empowering many others in opposite and equal value; you now know the rules of injustice.

Now you also know the rules of equality, freedom and true self-empowerment.

I AM RESPLENDENT

NOW CAN YOU SEE THE NEW ME?

Chapter Sixteen

I Am Injustice

NOW SEE ME

When doing platform, I was constantly accused of being sexist, bigoted and a man hater because I'd make the audience aware of the intense male injustices of the past and today. I'd relate my Adam and Eve theory and because old philosophies debate that synopsis and dictate the fault to be that of Eve as opposed to Adam it could create a misogynistic competitiveness within some groups.

To this day many ministers, male and female still swamp me with their derogatory arguments of god is love, the devil is hatred and these fear-boding super humans are responsible for all our life outcomes.

Through their egocentric apprehension, they don't really listen to me and they insinuate that I'm saying I don't believe in any God. I'm not saying that at all. I'm saying; the sending of the son theory, and the saving our ass theory has to be a fallacy, because the oneness of God was here long before we were and universe was absolutely perfect then and still is now, so we didn't need saving and never will.

It is our constant lack of personal responsibility that is the cause of our dire need to believe we need to be saved.

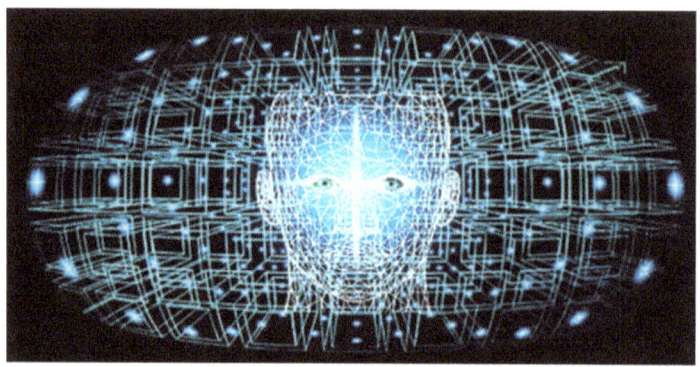

WE ALONE DESIGNED OUR STORIES

Cosmic-ally, all future paths have already been determined and because everything is perfect, they are highly successful. All your wants and needs have already been supplied and taken care of; no further assistance will ever be required. Pending your binary readings will determine where you end up. Your binary readings are determined by every thought, word, action and reaction you carry out now.

By screaming out for help is determining powerlessness, that's reacting and empowering some emotional injustice from your past to relive; that's your personal victimisation; That's everything God isn't.

God is oneness. Oneness is all emotions equally within as one. God is the perfect flat line. There is no judging nor interfering, that's emotional injustice: Your direction is your choice; however, every judicious choice has that wave of opposite and equal repercussion with the exact same value, good, bad or indifferent.

You can only understand the entire intensity of your answer to your query, by experiencing all the ramifications of your question.

If you need the Jesus ethos to exist within you, then by all means use it to assist you in your existence. However, you are emotionally empowering your fear into supremacy verses inferiority. Neither exist unless you want it to.

The magnificence of the universe is there, it's always there. Allow all you created for you to come to you in the manner it is supposed to, this way you achieve your highest benefit.

It is not there for the asking; when you ask you will receive, and to receive is to experience and to experience is to eventually understand. It just may take another 20000 years.

My God exists within me; It is the original "0" in the original binary of everything. It cannot leave me; it is every cell of me. No one can exist without it. This is my interpretation of what empowers me; you have yours; you create yours; it too is like a finger print. It is as individual as you are.

When you allow all the wonders of the universe come to you, they do, but not in chronological order. It's like a jigsaw puzzle. You only receive the pieces you need when you need them.

This creates an amazing attitude to life. You no longer suffer the stresses of the world. You realise you now have nothing to worry about. So, all you have to do now is live, create and enjoy.

In this new age we are discovering more tangible truths. Many young ones no longer require imaginary friends or crutches to gain their true inner perspective. Understanding how to empower their own future paths has to now be the tutelage for growth and development. We will evolve regardless, but wouldn't it be nice if we knew what we were doing?

You have to experience all that God isn't, to understand all that God is

The heinous religious philosophies of the past will NOT sustain the next generation in 5000 years' time.

This generation are not fighting for survival anymore; they do not need the titanic victimisations of some overpowering autocratic to exist. They have uncovered the truths and they will use those truths to empower themselves forward into a vibrant technological age.

There will be new evolutionary principles that will advance their existences through time. Principles based on proof through science, computerisation and facts. Facts that support non-victimisation and free enterprise. The evolution will take place with or without your feudal Vatican.

God is the 0 the neutral line of all things. It is in complete harmony with all things, non-divided. It is the nothingness yet everything of all things as one. It is the Nirvana of all things. It is the beginning and end of all things.

A little example to assist you with understanding. At 12 am there is nothing. One nano second past 12 you start entering the light of day. As each second passes you become closer to daylight. At 12 pm you reach the maximum. From that period on you start the regression back into night. As each nano second passes you journey closer. At the precise second of 12 am, for the next zero, zero, zero, to infinity for the briefest of moments, you are neither yesterday nor tomorrow, yet you are both. You aren't even a breath of the universe. You are the nothingness yet you are everything. Within that nothingness you hold the past present and future in your hands. You are the now of the everything in existence. However, we can still only realise this entire experience from our perception of time.

When you do not understand "love" as I didn't and suddenly you receive anything that makes you feel happy, you automatically interpret it as love and swallow it like a starving child. This is a natural reaction. So, after sixty odd years, I had to ask, what do you call a love that it is sadistic and victimising yet still presumed as love.

When you undergo a life between life transition or NDE, there is this amazing feeling of supposed love that overwhelms us, but it is not love. It is the oneness, the completeness, the harmony, quiet, the flatline of all things enveloping us, as it is supposed to be. This is who we are when we connect to our oneness.

How do I know it is not love.? Because like everything else, *we create* our perception of love. It is simply another emotion we have fabricated from our awareness of something we need to feel within us.

Same as our interpretation of hate. There are 7 billion people in the world today and they all have different ratios of the emotion of hate within them. My binary code of hate is completely different to yours by a small micro-nano emotion, just like a fingerprint. So, for anyone to say that "God is love" is only interpreting some emotional experience from their perspective. However, the word for that emotion does not exist, for it is different for everyone; but the feelings of that word within everyone is very real.

All your existences to date are founded on all your verbal expressions against the emotional injustices that you have experienced in your past lives. They are then re-experienced at the same ratio that you have expressed them.

"What you said then, is now, exactly what you are experiencing and what you physically look like."

You may have lashed out at others against discrimination; but the verbal terminology you used has been emotionally recorded in your binary, word for emotional word, according to your interpretation of that word. Your DNA then instantly formulates your future timelines from your feelings. The more intensely you verbally empower that feeling, the more it amplifies, expands, evolves and immediately starts to alter your physical appearance.

All those verbal expressions physically define you and others as humans. From the beginning of man's time, billions and billions of cells have physically transformed everyone's body through those emotional words, to appear as their physical interpretation of that emotion of injustice in very lifetime. That's why you are fat, skinny or bald.

Confrontations are the best way to discover the words you used in your past that have designed your physical appearance today. The more intense the confrontation the more baggage you are carrying. Words like "Are you stupid? Or are you blind or something?" could indicate your feelings of injustice to being treated as inferior.

Confrontations are only others informing you of the victimised verbal abuse that you are physically wearing; bad health, that rickety knee, that painful back. They are all expressions of the verbal abuse from your past life that you used on others and now you are wearing as your physical garment.

Now you recognise what that specific injustice physically appears like; you are wearing it. However, now you also understand, that by registering the injustice within you, you know *what justice isn't*.

You and the boisterous advocate are re-living a past moment. He is displaying your past path of injustice from victimising mode, and you are displaying his past life from victim mode. The path victimises all contenders.

You can now remain in victim mode and continue the on the same path by reacting or recognise your AHA moment and choose freedom.

So far, I have spoken about reincarnation from the perspective of the individual but an amazing alteration can occur in mass as well.

The story of Hoover is a generic tale based on an incident that occurred about six years ago. It was a small seminar 20- 30 people and it was based on our hypnosis research of immortality and understanding death. This took place about two years after we uncovered the real path of suicide, miscarriages and cot death. We, as a group, were sharing our results with others at seminars.

Our very young female speaker was testing her ability on the floor discussing the impact of suicide when a huge well-built male audience member sat forward in his seat and literally confronted her. My first impression was, he appeared to have attended the seminar with the intention raising a ruckus.

"How do you know this shit? How can you teach it when you know nothing about it?" He was referring to our research on suicide. I was in the audience and after a period, I could see our young speaker was having difficulty, for this arrogant intruder was determined to not only disrupt her oration, he was being a smart ass and wanted to stress her as a speaker and he succeeded.

Big John wasn't available this day and he usually controls the audience. Other members of the audience supported the young lass and tried to defuse the situation, but he was determined to own the floor and was enjoying his ability to take advantage of the situation.

I waited for a period of time, probably hoping it would subside but it didn't, then when my gut could not handle any more of his insults, I stepped up, the same way John would have.

I asked the young lass if she knew the answers to the man's debarkle and she shied away almost relieved that I stood up. I asked her to take a seat while I tried to defuse his situation. I borrowed the young girl's microphone and asked the abuser for his name.

"Who are you?" was his indignant response, as he poked his face at me hoping to achieve the same control over me.

Feeling both insulted and sarcastic and wanting to take back the floor, my ego and fight for survival spoke for itself. "Well do you want me to call you Hoover? I paused; then he responded. "Allan"

"Now would you sit back quietly please Allan." Some laughed, but he was not impressed as I stood quietly and stared at him eye to eye; then the young woman beside him pulled him back into this seat.

Firstly, I re-addressed the audience to help them understand the path put before them by the previous speaker. Then I challenged the agitated audience member who was being asked by other audience members to leave and he stated he had a right to stay.

I introduced a new piece of information not discussed before. "This entire exercise was being re-lived now by everyone here present, it's not just for Allan. It involves each and every one of us."

I paced back and forth as I do when I speak and felt I my rhythm return, so I continued. "The first part of this lesson is to understand that you create all your existences *for* your own experiences only; and you also create all your existences *from* your own experiences only. You help no one; you harm no one; and everything you think, do, and say, is entirely for you, to experience, no one else. You create all of it."

Allan put forth the logical argument, from his perspective, "if someone murdered another person, they are physically harming that person."

I had to return to the beginning, to help them all comprehend that it was the other way around. I had to justify that the murdered person was already walking a that path long before they were slain. This was a synopsis never explained to this group before.

"Through your appraisal, good or bad, of a murder of similar value in your past life, you emotionally reacted to the injustice; this is because the binaries of both contenders already matched due to that appraisal. By reacting, you now become a part of that same timeline and now have to experience that same murder in exactly the same way.

These binary codes are a response to that appraisal and that appraisal only. Your question was the same question the murderer asked in his previous existence and the answer has only one destination; this specific type of murder.

Instantly within you, your binary codes and your genetic codes alter so you can personally experience every emotion of injustice demanded for you to achieve the final goal, which will be your murder."

I continued. "Karma equals opposite and equal value. Your interpretation of the how the murder took place, you record, according to your belief systems, your personal values at that time and from those values you walk this same future murderous path.

For example; you may have witnessed the murder by beheading during the French Revolution, so your feelings of that experience would be different to the genocide of women and children during the crusades; or would they? The scenery may be different, but your emotional and verbal opinion **is** the embodiment of you.

Then if you were a soldier fighting for king and pope and you were raping innocent women, children and babies and pillaging in your God's name, what would your feelings of this experience be? Exactly the same feelings of injustice; however, the emotional intent is different.

The emotional feelings in fighting against king and pope in the revolution to save the starving people, is an emotion of victimisation against the powerful. Your fight for God, king and country is for the powerful over the weak, the injustice is the same; however, with each new existence the emotional intent alters and evolves; now you have to re-live your emotion of injustice through this new emotional feeling. Your scenery has altered, the purpose has altered but your embodiment of injustice hasn't.

You have, through all your existences, physically evolved as the emotional embodiment of your feeling of injustice. Every life time, with every new reaction, a new emotional will be added to your injustice thus the new experience will commence.

Through asking or reacting, you will experience every single one of them till you eventually understand that true justice is not asking. True justice is allowing.

It's not the popes nor the people; it's you behind the fight. You've given it some emotional name of justice or injustice but neither name exists. You are the physical embodiment of all your emotional injustices.

So, you will experience all paths of injustice not due to justice or injustice but due to your inner emotional values; your feelings, your opinions. You have allowed these emotional opinions within you to define you and determine all your paths. They control you; you are their victim, you control nothing.

Here today before you all, is the perfect situation of this very same synopsis. Before you all here today, is a man who is already on the same path as his suicidal victim due to his past feelings of emotional injustice.

I looked him straight in the eye and asked. May I ask, friend or family?" There was a long pause.

His friend took his hand and answered for him "His nephew."

"My condolences," I offered but continued.

"This gentleman is now exposing his pain for us to see his injustice You hear his words, you see his actions, you physically see this man. What you do not see is the embodiment of him as the emotion of injustice. What you also do not see is that same injustice is reflected in all of you. That's why you are here. That's why I'm here. We all reflect him and each other.

His other emotions are also within us but at different ratios. Anger, hurt, probably confused; but his path just like ours is definitely one of emotional injustice again.

For me to say that, you all created all this, is the last thing you all want to hear, but it is true.

"Another thing that I haven't mentioned is; this boy, your nephew wasn't always your nephew. However, when you assessed the original barbarism of this incident two maybe three centuries ago, it probably involved some emotional impact between a father and a son; an uncle and nephew; in the case of a suicide, a mass suicide, a murder or a war.

In this situation, you deemed yourself as judge. More educated than; more civil than and you judged from your feelings of justice and injustice, superior verses inferior

You questioned; we all questioned; now you must experience all there is to know of what justice isn't. So, for many lifetimes you have experienced all there is to know about the path of many different injustices and suicide is just another path. This particular combination of various emotions along with your embodiment of injustice results in only one path, suicide.

Now you are being answered. Simple as that and as horrid as that. You asked for justice. "Ask and you shall receive." However, due to karma, you will always receive your justice in the opposite and equal value for you to understand.

You can only use the emotional tools you provided, for you to use; injustice, hatred anger rage abandonment loneliness, loss, however, the names do not exist, only your feelings of the emotions do and they are what you used. How you use them is what gives you your final result. *Reacting to you journey only continues the journey; responding and allowing your journey can alter your journey.*

What everyone here has to understand now is, this emotional trauma is now being re-lived at this moment by all of us. His emotional feelings are now activating those same feelings of emotional injustice within you. You, now through your judgement of Allan's experience are doing exactly the same as what he did in his past. You are empowering different feelings to enhance your injustice, new ones to experience again.

Your reactions or responses to these activations will define you personally as well as your future paths.

This entire incident here today, is an experience of feedback for all of us. We are all reliving this past life occurrence at this moment. However, if you react as Allan did in his past, you too will face the same traumatic experience he has had to suffer for lifetimes to the end or, you can let it go now. Allan has the same choice.

How? By realising that this path of injustice that you physically embody as a human being is simply a path; but it is actually vicitmising you.

It is not the suicide that is the driving force. It is you. You are dressed as your garment of injustice. You are injustice, and as such, you match all other binaries of injustice to experience.

The suicide is simply another vehicle of choice. What is being explained here as your feedback; if you wish to experience this form of toxic emotional injustice or trauma to its fullest, this is what it looks like and this is how it travels and this is how ends; very specific.

It is feedback only. This particular desired injustice this gentleman is feeling, has only one path but within it are billions of different variables of injustice for him to experience over many life times.

Your nephew in this life, was on the same path ahead of you. He like you, judged a similar incident before you, maybe twenty years prior. Then you did the same thing and started your own timeline following in his footsteps. The default program is, this form of noxious emotional injustice will always lead to suicide.

Basically, you were both living your lives and became distracted by the injustice of a traumatic situation and reacted to it and questioned the injustice

Once you assume judgement; once you again fight for justice or injustice; you don't have the choice whether you wish to experience it or not. When you assume superiority, query, or question something, you literally jump into the whirlpool of that story, then experience it to the end.

That's the continuum of reincarnation that's the time line to history repeating itself. Each story doesn't stop until you finish it. You can keep empowering it with every existence and remain its victim for as long as you like. You can re-empower it again today by reacting to your emotional stress which is again screaming injustice. This is a final vital predetermined component of the reactionary path that is needed for you to lead you to that final outcome.

Now here is the challenge before all of us.

All of us are here today because our binaries match and we are all wearing the same garment of injustice; the only variance is our emotional ratios.

If you too want to know the answer to this injustice, then you too can follow suit to the endgame of committing suicide for this path has just been offered to you and it has only one direction.

The path you are experiencing is both the original question of injustice you used to accuse with and the final feeling you are experiencing now. It is the same injustice in answer to your accusation.

The embodiment of injustice is you; It's us, just different variances, like everyone in this room. They all appear different due to the variation of the emotional variances That is what your audience is telling you; and that is what you are telling them. You are one and the same.

Now you know. This feeling of injustice has been your journey for centuries, building you, upgrading you, evolving you, preparing you for this final experience. Understanding what the true justice is.

You didn't do this to hurt you. It was all done to give you the answer to a situation you didn't fully understand; to a situation that imprisoned you for centuries. Now hopefully you do understand, so now you can let it all go, or you will find out how entire story ends.

The point is, your feelings of injustice kept defining you as a human being. By continually empowering it over and over again you evolved imprisoning yourself, creating this ongoing victim within you. It was never the circumstances.

In one lifetime you express it as perpetrator the next as victim, but always injustice, always the victim. This is your dilemma. You have divided the emotion of injustice to into billions of emotions to understand all there is to know about justice.

Every lifetime you are empowering one more component of injustice against another emotional component of injustice from existence to existence so it could balance, but it always was injustice.

This time your injustice embodiment entails victimising others with bullying, arrogance, dominance, denigration. How do I know? Because you just displayed all those emotions before all of us? These feelings personify you; not your situation.

But within you is the opposite and equal balancing effect of karma. Abandonment, aloneness, feelings of isolation, sadness despair; you will be feeling many of these as well and if you continue, this will be your new embodiment of emotional despair.

This is your feedback. If you maintain focus on these emotions, if you empower them, they will upgrade, enlarge and physically personify your future path to your suicide, for this is its deemed victimised path.

HOWEVER!

Now all of us can choose. As I said we are all re-living this and Allan is appearing before us as victim. You are before him because your binary codes are displaying that same imprisoning format. You have been informed of what emotion governs Allan and why he arrived here this morning and invariably bought you and me here because we match.

You have all seen the answers to the old path, you all know how this will end. You've all seen its results and it is all thanks to you Allan. So, he is extremely important to you at this moment.

Allan's experience may have saved all of us from following this traumatic emotional path. The more you speak of it through your desperate feelings of it, the more people you ask to join you on your painful journey through their emotional paths of injustice; but now none of us have to. It's over. We can make new choices.

The beautiful person who portrayed your nephew in this life, exposed to you all those answers. He was victim. You now are the same as him, you are victim. Can you see that? You need to be able to see that; for then you will realise that every component of all your past lives regarding this situation was revealed to you through your nephew.

All of this was essential for all of us to completely understand the magnificence of the freedom of the justice we all gave us to truly experience. You cannot achieve this awareness until you have experienced every essence of this injustice with all its extreme variances in all situations.

Be grateful to your nephew, thank him, love him, and if you wish to follow him enjoy your journey, for it is simply an answer not a punishment.

But should you choose another path, a better path, look at how many other lives you have saved here today as well.

You empowered your emotion of injustice over others; we all do. You divided your house, we all do, as a result we all have to continually re-balance our house.

Hopefully now we can see the victimisation this path offers. Then if we can, we are also able to see the freedom it offers as well, for they are one.

By allowing the injustice to remain the injustice for it informs you of what injustice is, you can equalise it with your justice. You no longer empower one emotion over the other but utilise them both equally, eliminating all forms of victimisation.

You are equalising your binary of justice and injustice as equal to each other for now neither exist. Neither have power. For every justice there is an automatic injustice of equal value everywhere around you, balanced. Now you will transform physically into a new person of equality.

By doing that you create equality within you and because you and all these magnificent beings are one, you here today will match their binaries also. Instead of all of them following you to a timeline of destruction, you through your inner ability to create equality within you have freed them. Now like you, they have to realise the universe already has supplied them with all the justice love and equality they ever require so they need never ask. It's already been taken care of. They like you just have to learn how to allow and not question.

What that means now in every life time at this time with the same information and with the same impact you and every one of these people here today will experience and huge feeling of emancipation. That's a wonderful gift Allan, and you could not have done that without the assistance of your nephew.

Everything is perfect and will always be. You don't need to ask for anything.

For the record Allan your nephew finished his path and cleaned his slate. Now he is a new soul with a brand-new life to experience of his choosing. They usually return to their original path before they got distracted and continue life with their original loved ones. He too is no longer a victim, he's happy again. Now if you accept his gift, you will have the same if not better path.

I put the microphone back on the podium. I walked back to my seat. The young lass picked up her microphone and was content to continue her performance. It was an exceptional day and a lot was achieved.

After the meeting we had coffee and Allan's friend thanked me, but Allan had left. I collected my bag and left.

At the seminar as a group, we were all experiencing our past life regression together. I had always taught this from the individual perspective, but this was the first time I entertained it as a group, as a nation, or as a world.

AT some stage in our past lives all of us experienced this same occurrence, only I was listening instead of speaking. The speaker, the teacher said word for word what I said. That's why the information flowed.

The reverberations of that timeline echoed through our mirror to this lifetime at that exact same time for us all to re-experience. Now we all altered our binary to equality and freedom have created our new echo and it is coming to all of us. We do not have to chase it. We already have it; we simply have to allow it.

Everything we do in this life is a re-living regression of our past lives through karma; What happened then is still occurring now; the timing, the words, the impacts. It is an ongoing continuum going up and down and re-enacting the same dramas with injustice variances. This is our history repeating itself and we keep repeating it till we stop. It is our reactions to each experience that determines our path of our future timelines.

Ask and you WILL receive it.

but you never have to;

You already gave yourself everything you will ever need.

NOW I SEE ALL MY PATHS.

PAST AND FUTURE

I WAS INJUSTICE.

NOW I SEE ME.

Chapter Seventeen

I WAS BLIND

NOW SEE ME

As Rabindranath Tagore stated in 1950, "DO NOT TEACH YOUR CHILDREN YOUR PATH, FOR THEY ARE FAR MORE ADVANCED THAN YOU."

Your children are ***your*** future, not your past.

The ongoing continuum is a fluctuating wave of highs and lows. Your past and future mirror each other at the top of your graph and you are in between them at the bottom where you echo and experience both of them.

These teachings were shown to the old men of yore but were shunned as occultism or mysticism and the teachers were either excommunicated, imprisoned or extinguished.

Today for the first time in history women have rights, real rights. We are allowed to stand up to authority without being killed maimed or abused. We are allowed to question authority. We are allowed to be empowered as women and stand tall among our adversaries. We are allowed to be real women, not women in a man's world.

We are allowed to discover and create the genuine truth. A truth that shows us that everything that has ever been taught to us over the last 200000 years is a lie, but a necessary evil, so we can determine the fractured psyche that created us. Now we can choose freedom due to our understanding of that pain. It gives us options for a more productive future for all.

The reason we couldn't advance past nuclear weaponry is because the binary of Adam was still enforcing our inner need to survive mode. His fighting warrior modes of yore; Man keeps re-living this ongoing emotional regression of history repeating itself from that original egocentric survival instinct.

Karmic clique; If you pull a trigger; expect to be shot.

Our children do not have to exist with that ongoing tyranny. Our children do not have to exist and maintain the teachings of old men's egos, fears, lies and petty power plays that will eventually lead to human-wide extinction.

If we are to have a better more responsible future, we have to let the young show us the way. First of all, we have to relinquish the bindings that are restricting them. Teach them the impossible doesn't exist because they have already conquered it.

Then allow their creativity to flow to them, flow through them. Allow them to fly and if you have the courage, follow.

Their story of the world they live in is alive and free. There are no restrictions, there is no segregation, or separation. Their world is full of wonderment and possibilities.

The reality of the old man's world is based on the opposite of emotional injustices inequality discriminations biases of unequal value.

The young one's world is full of life and vitality also generosity and mind-boggling fun, laughter, happiness, joy and prosperity for everyone equally.

If a child is disabled, the very young will help them naturally. If they are coloured or of another ethnic descent, the very young will hold their hand and skip with them. There is no discrimination or racial segregation in the mind of the young. There are no bombs. There is no hatred. There is no radiation that will not only destroy all their land but all inhabitants as well.

The young will cry because old men are killing the innocent in the world. Why don't old men cry? They really should.

The old men say, *"these are but children and do not know the ways of the real world."*

The sad retort to that answer is; *"we know. But you will soon teach them the art of fear and hate won't you? Pity that!"*

However, what if we decided not to teach them your cold hearted, educated civilised, frozen, judgemental buffoonery. What if we gave them another option; a means to neutralise all the nuclear waste and radiation you have left behind you as your civilised legacy?

For centuries upon centuries we have experienced denigration, abuse, defamation and violence because the first derogatory men Adam believed themselves to be like some superficial God of power due to their titanic strength and ability to annihilate and eradicate all life forms on earth to extinction; firstly, to survive, then, in later centuries simply because they could. In their vanity of supremacy, they refused to allow others to question their authority; they would be vanquished. Their word was their ever-powerful bond.

From this standpoint the warrior claimed allegiances with a mighty God; but it wasn't. From his myths and legends, we are informed how he assumed he would ordain more mightier powers, if he pleased his Gods.

Unbeknownst to him, he utilised the same laws of the universe to create his future timelines as you do today to create yours. He too for centuries walked the path of his emotional injustices to the fullest. He too reacted from his self-worth of superior or inferior feelings. Believing himself to be powerful justice, he deemed upon his world endless paths of injustices from his authoritative position thus empowering his and our ongoing karmic path of opposite and equal effect.

To this day everything they created can also be justified in our world. We are Adam's descendants; their binary is synchronised with ours. Our binaries match the binaries of their belief systems to comply with their injustices. Everything they testified to, they recorded in their binary. Every experience that occurred during their lifetime you are experiencing through live regression in one form or another. Everything around you is a product of all his victimisation exposed before you.

Today, still, every injustice within every individual was instilled with the same attitude from that original default binary of 0 and 011+. That original egocentric instinct of survival.

Adam's generation imparted mass displays of injustice to empower themselves individually. The results then brandished were future paths of isolation, bigotry, sexism, racism, prejudice, chauvinism, narrow-mindedness, brutality, violence and death.

For the past 20000 centuries Adam has had one heinous card up his sleeve, and it has been used at every opportunity through our binaries. His fear instinct, his questioning instinct.

From early childhood I have always questioned why women were treated the way they were treated and why didn't we stand up against the abuse. And why men were allowed to be abusive and why I had to go to school?

The legacy from the1970's women was *"to allow their education to stand for something"* We saw our future potential was already there; we just have to allow us to have it. We, however, are still allowing men to give us *their* freedom, but it has conditions.

We are allowed to use our new education to further advance ourselves, far further than man ever could. That Prime Minister of 1972 liberated women, empowering them and all Australian's equally, and that small keyhole of advancement, although still very small, will never be closed.

Little did he know he opened the door to a new breed of woman, man and child.

My Eve is like that Prime Minister. My inevitable path has already been determined. It is more than I ever conceived possible. I don't have to ask, question, or judge. Everything will be provided in the most emancipating manner.

I know what Adam achieved. It is exposed around me every day. I know my past history of him, I see my present history of him. I know what he looks like, what he acts like and how his path ends. What's more I now also know how he feels.

I do not know why I was allowed to be educated in this century and not earlier, but I do now know that the by re-experiencing all the noxious educated dogmas of the past I comprehend that they are all incorrect and in understanding that, I have opened the door to what the truth is. I understand I need both to advance forward.

Now as truly educated women and children we can find ways to stop the continued barbarism and cease all nuclear warfare and achieve peace? How? By knowing we have already created it; by knowing all we have to do is allow it. By knowing not to ask for it or question it.

By allowing our new and miraculous path to come to us, we will conquer the unconquerable.

All the continent leaders of the world have this choice. They can continue on their vicitmised path of destined destruction and destroy the entire world or they can choose to acknowledge that this ongoing disastrous situation of their making due to their old demoralised belief systems, is not the answer.

However, now the true predicament is; the old generation truly do not believe they are victims. They still believe their God will save them. They don't know how to render it. It's easier to pass the buck to the others and take no responsibility.

> The young are still fighting the civilised educated constituents of society who only have one goal in mind. $$$$$$$$$$

TEACH OUR CHILDREN WELL.

We are still fighting the fights we fought back then, but now we don't have to. Now we understand their real purpose. The fights are to teach us what justice isn't.

THEIR NEW PATH has already been concreted. You could say the gaseous path for the future fire has been paved, it is simply a new timeline that has to be travelled and re-lived again and again and again.

However, if we educated and empowered our young correctly, they will create new belief systems that propose newer brighter possibilities. They will adapt the entrepreneurial attitude of endless possibilities of successes. They will find real dreams that will surge them forward and never stop.

There are several young children in Australia now under fifteen who have started successful internet businesses. Now is the time. We have new tools, new knowledge, new options, new opportunities and the internet doesn't care who, how or what you look like. It's neutral, equal and well equipped. It's awaiting brilliant minds and creators.

This new surge of empowerment will be boundless, energetic and upgrading continuously. No sooner will they develop one idea when the next brainwave is forming in their heads ready for market to enhance all lives equally. They are allowing their dreams to come to them and pave their futures.

This is where Adam's fail. Their fear tires them; they get old and want to stop. They start fearing change, they want to settle down. Let them. Continue without them, but don't stop, and don't let them stop you; fly forever.

This is our new true evolutionary path of the future. Not the strongest shall survive, but the most genius and creative shall fly and not be touched by the old generic world of fear and injustice.

The aged and dogmatic will complain of the injustice for they will feel victimised and be left behind. The civilised educated old governments will double your taxes for they too no longer know how to contribute. But like the wisdom from the Aborigines and the Indians three hundred years ago, the young will again be able to say to the educated civilised white man;

YOU WERE WARNED!

The brilliance of an entrepreneur's dream outshines all arrogance of white man capitalism. No sooner had Bill Gates developed the latest model when he was allowing the next upgrade. It would be better more efficient more exciting. Walt Disney wanted something more and bigger and better for everyone to enjoy; he went to worldwide. They allowed the dream to empower them; they allowed their dreams to embody them

The stories of their lives were ones without restrictions and imprisoning binds of, "you can't do that!" Their response was "why not, let's find out. Let's find a way to do it." and they did it, over and over again.

This didn't make them exceptional; they didn't ask, they allowed. Their non-victimised attitude to life was the driving force that made them spontaneous and different from the average fearful Joe. This is what made them more dynamic and exciting.

Their passion for their creativeness; this is what they enjoyed most. They allowed their dreams to come to them and it gave them the tenacity to move through all the binds of Adam's apathetic attitudes to life. The more they created, the more they wanted to create. The more they wanted to create the faster the upgrades came, the faster newer ideas exploded into their reality.

When you are caught in the quagmire of stagnancy it is like trying to push a broken billy cart up a craggy stonewall staircase. You cannot see in front of you and there is only one direction, round and round in circles.

When you allow and you are in creative mode, it is as if you are flying high above the earth in a jet. You are travelling at extremely high speeds but you don't feel you are moving. You see all that is around you in every direction. You can make better choices and more dynamic decisions. You have higher, wider perspective and visuals and your conception reveals a much higher awareness.

Imagine futures created by these dynamic minds and attitudes.

They don't ask; they know it all has already been created and resolved; therefore, they have nothing to worry about, fret about; they appreciate everything and everyone equally. They materialise the successful holographic future already preordained. A flourishing future for all to exist in and live in peace, harmony and good health.

Because all are productive, all will have the wealth they need automatically; a world free of struggle and poverty, this is what the universe offers.

Enough is enough! Let the aged experience their desiccation. Let their questions be answered and experienced. It is time for a change.

Man-made narcissistic questions have done their course and explained what allowance isn't. It has given us this world of wars, injustice, prejudice, bigotry, racism, sexism, brutality, murder, hatred, impoverishment of humans, land, animals and minerals all for money.

Now we have experienced it, all of it to the full,
we understand we can now choose

ALLOWANCE.

Our leaders are giving us the feedback of our past as they mirror our future. They are giving us more of the same. Although they speak in terms of a better futures, they cannot produce it, for in their very presence of mind they deem a path from the same arrogance and ignorance they created it. Yet, they have the audacity to exult in their civil supremacy of continued war mongering treachery. It is their very deceitful civility that deems their continued failure.

We have learnt our lessons, visible and invisible. We owe nothing. We owe our neighbours nothing. We owe the world nothing and we owe your God nothing.

> In understanding this, we now have the most vital gift to ever exist in the palm of our hands.

EVERYTHING

> Adam and Eve lived 200000 years of imprisoned injustice. We had to experience all of it to understand all that we aren't; so, we now know who we are.

I'm constantly informed that I'm bigoted, sexist and a man hater and it is usually men informing me of this great exposure.

For years my response was "out of the mouths of the accuser."

Now days with more self-confidence I stand my ground and ask them

Let's turn the cards the other way round. Let's put the shoe on the other foot.

Two hundred thousand years ago, I took control, as a woman. I was the one who fought and destroyed all existence thus becoming the invincible supreme woman head. God was all woman

From that standpoint on, you became my property and should you ever question my authority you would be abused horrendously, castrated, burned to the stake or drowned.

You were never allowed to be treated with respect for you were equivalent to the cattle. The only thing you were good for was creating more female spawn.

I created doctrines and laws that for centuries allowed me to take away all your rights, your land, your homes, your dignity. You owned nothing; you never will, not even you name. Women were allowed to rape and murder you because you were worthless and soul less barbarians, below me; inferior.

Instead of having all your food laid out on a beautiful table, you had to grapple for it where ever you could, because we women liked our parties and you as our dogs.

200000 years of this and then one day, someone says to you, "you are free; you are equal." How would that feel? That's how we feel.

For the first time in over 200000 years, we as women are allowed to be whoever we want; do whatever we want; go where ever we want; become whomever we want and no one is allowed harm us.

I could waste my time and become vicitmised again or I can choose to become the best of both of worlds. Oneness means the uniting of all component of me together as one. My Eve and my Adam; then energising both of them to that newer force of empowerment. This is to prevent me from slipping again.

I don't know how many centuries I have been dreaming of this moment. I don't know how many paths I've had to take to arrive here. But I know every one of them was important. Now I understand that and by empowering all my vicitmised injustices within me with my emancipating emotions of freedom within me I no longer walk the waved line of karma's dividedness.

My line is straight, pure, and true. It has only one direction, forwards.

I cannot ask you to join me that is your decision, and if you want to stay where you are that is also allowed.

All I ask is you display the same respect to me as I share with you. You do not have the right to victimise me or insult me because I no longer wish to play with you.

For me, I have never been happier in any existence, and as such, I transform with every thought word and deed. My future experiences have already been ordained and will be expressed in the same and equal proportion for my karmic line is straight and equal.

THE AMAZING WORLD YOU WISH TO
RETURN TO ALREADY EXISTS.

ALLOW THAT WORLD YOU WISH TO RETURN TO,

TO COME TO YOU:

NOW I SEE

NOW YOU SEE ALL OF ME;
MY WORLDS; MY ENVIRONMENTS;

I HAVE TO EXPERIENCE THE
NOTHINGNESS OF EVERYTHING

TO UNDERSTAND THE EVERYTHING OF
NIRVANA

Chapter Eighteen

REINCARNATIONAL CONTINUUM

HISTORY REPEATING ITSELF.

EVERY THOUGHT WORD AND ACTION THAT YOU GENERATE EMBODIES YOU AS A PERSON.

EVERY EMOTION YOU PURVEY BE IT HATRED, RACISM, SEXISM, THEFT, GENOCIDE; IT WILL BE RETURNED TO YOU IN THE SAME AND EQUAL VALUE.

KARMA STATES YOU WILL RECEIVE ALL IN OPPOSITE EFFECT AND OF EQUAL VALUE.

THE WORLD WILL EVOLVE; AND YOUR UNJUSTIFIABLE ACTIONS MAY BE REPAIRED AS THE WORLD MOVES ON. HOWEVER, YOUR UNDERLYING UNACCEPTABLE BEHAVIOUR CARRIED OUT BY YOU, WILL REINARNATE AS YOU.

YOU MAY NOT RETURN FOR TWO THOUSAND YEARS, AND THE ENTIRE ENVIRONMENT OF THE WORLD WILL HAVE

ALTERED. HOWEVER, YOUR BINARIES WILL DETERMINE THAT YOU BE RETURNED TO THE SAME SITUATION YOU CREATED IN YOUR PAST LIFE, AS THE RECIPIENT, TO RE-EXPERIENCE YOUR NEW EMOTIONAL INJUSTICE.

THIS IS HISTORY REPEATING ITSELF; THIS IS YOU REPEATING YOUR HISTORY

IT WILL NEVER STOP; UNTIL YOU STOP IT. YOU ARE WARNED EVERY EXISTENCE; YOU ALWAYS HAVE FREEDOM OF CHOICE.

THIS WASN'T A PERSONAL FIGHT AGAINST YOU: IT WAS A PERSONAL FIGHT CREATED BY YOU.

YOUR PAST LIFE HISTORY CREATE YOUR FUTURE TIMELINES;

ALLOWING GIVES YOU YOUR FUTURE LIVES IN ABUNDANCE:

Now Can You See Me?

YOU WILL.

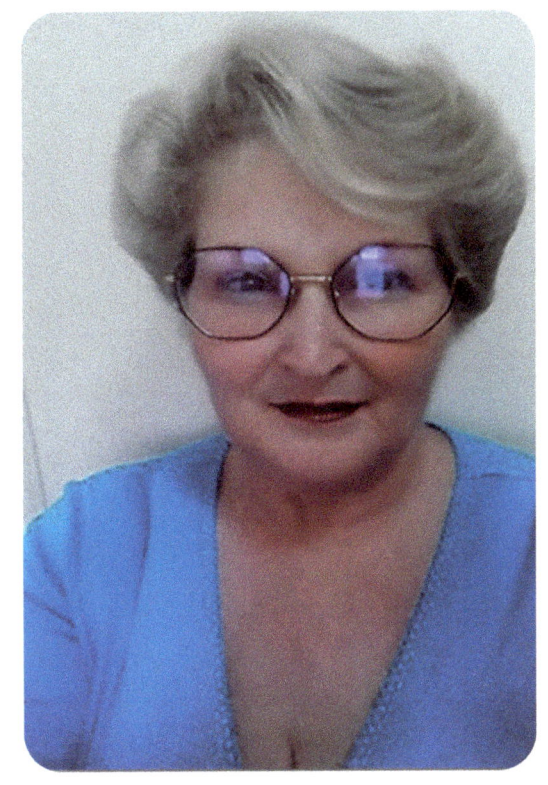

I AM GAYLE

Index Of Images Pixabay

woman-3509143__340 network pixabay page 14

woman-2997991__340 fantasy landscape pixabay

woman-1446557__480network pixabay page 1

woman-641528__340 fantasy landscape woman

futuristic-3862179__340 fantasy 24 pixabay

 universe-3898921__340 person galaxy pixabay page 14.jpg

 universe-2736507__340 and space pixabay page 2

 universe-1351865__340 and space pixabay page 2

 technology-3762549__340 pixabay brainwave

 Spirituality-Best-Wallpaper-23303 awakening baltana free downloads

 robot-3826558__340 cyborg network pixabay page 14

 hand-784077__340 puppeteer pixabay page 1)

 popart-3464230__340 matrix art pixabay

 mirroring-2968596__340 globe pixabay page 25

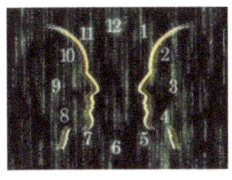 matrix-69681__340 face silhouette matrix data pixabay

 love-3527017__340pixabay kiss

 Indian-538442__340-person vintage pixabay 1

 infinity-3066212_1280 pixabay

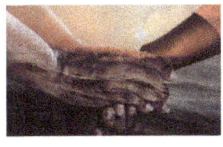 hands-2888625__340handshake pixabay page jpg

 galaxy-2852053__340 cosmic page 3

 fantasy-3281795__340clouds woman spirituality 2pixabay

 fantasy-2437944_1280transcendence pixabay dreaming

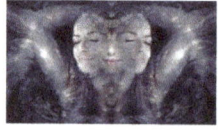 fantasy-2424681__340portrait pixabay surreal and fantasy page 2

 elephant composing-4421256__340 magical pixabay page 2

 earth-2765479__340 earth family cosmos

 digitization-2170795__340 network pixabay page 21

digitization- network pixabay page 13

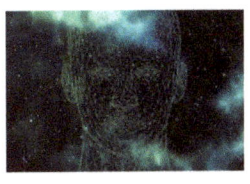

digitization-3552263__340 head pixabay page 2

children-2860024__340 heart in hand pixabay

binary-3175073__340 code matrix data image pixabay

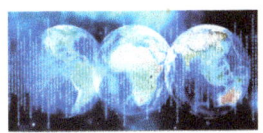

binary-1695475__340 code world pixabay page3

binary-1327501__340 code woman faces binary cade pixabay

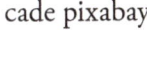
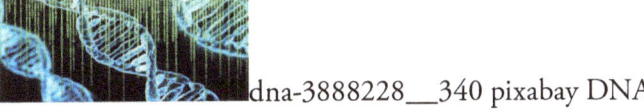

dna-3888228__340 pixabay DNA

 time-624686__340 clock abstract globe pixabay page 6

 baby-3758363__340 dream fantasy pixabay page 10

 atom-1222516__340pixabay radioactive page 1

 atom-1222513__340 pixabay nuclear page 1.jpg

 astronomy-3101270__340explosion pixabay

 astral-traveler-3715079__340 astral pixabay.jp

 arrangement-2794696__340vibrations   pixabay butterfly arrangement

 abstract-2732988__340picture pixabay galaxy page 3

 abstract-2170219__340shattered world pixabay page 3

 arrangement-663374__340pixabay arrangements aesthetics vibrations

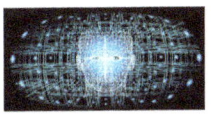 artificial-intelligence-4115193__340 network pixabay page 6

 binary-3044663__340one null space binary pixabay

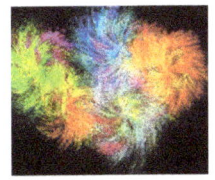 color-game-2080532__340 abstract fantasy 55 pixabay

 decorated-1297972__340 pixabay decorated key (2)

 family-2112266__340 love rainbow pixabay page 2

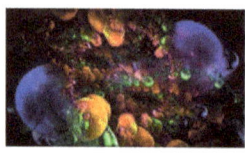 fractal-292056__340 art fantasy 12 pixabay

240_F_158665720_VyuY2XB052U8KxNOLhBXYUkapoFEg6k1Iceberg pixabay

www.ingramcontent.com/pod-product-compliance
Lightning Source LLC
Chambersburg PA
CBHW042111120526
44592CB00042B/2695